Uncharted

Thom Slade & M.T. Lisle

ISBN-13: 9781795579025

DEDICATION

This book is dedicated to all those feeling lost and alone on their divorce journey. No matter the mountain or sea monster, know that through the painful end, you can start a positive new beginning.

CONTENTS

ACKNOWLEDGMENTS

Thom – I would like to thank my family and friends (a special shout out to Veronica, Cary & Darren), Grandparents and of course God. Without you all, the journey would have been smaller, longer, darker and nowhere near as fun.
Also, to those that started and finished their journey too soon. Jim, you are missed and loved.

M.T. Lisle – I am so grateful to those who stuck by me, those friends and family I can call and pick up right where we left off. My mom, my dad, B, Delbrak, one crazy Georgian, my favorite boss, and my crew. Thanks more than my heart can take to my kids who make me a better person. Thank you for being my people.

Thom Slade & M.T. Lisle

FOREWORD & TRAVEL GUIDE

This book is not a "get out of jail free" card or a shortcut to passing "Go" with a $200 paycheck. Divorce sucks. Moving on to become a better you requires a long hard journey filled with all kinds of monsters and temptations. Our book is a simple and lighthearted journey guided by two seasoned travelers, a *His* and *Hers* post-divorce perspective of common obstacles and trials you'll likely encounter along the way. At the end of each chapter comes a simple postcard to yourself for personal goals, thoughts, or ideas you may have found helpful.

We all start from the cliff of separation, but from there we each choose our direction. Feel free to follow us on our course or choose a chapter that speaks more to your current situation. Either way, we all have the goal of reaching our personal post-divorce nirvana.

A New Journey Begins

Thom Slade & M.T. Lisle

CHAPTER 1 - THE END

One day we walked together and came to a cliff.

The cliff was as tall as the white cliffs of Dover, the sky a clear blue with drifting white clouds drawn by a gentle breeze. As we stood there on the edge looking out to the curve of the world and the outline of distant shores, our path became two. We could no longer move forward, but instead two paths now lead in directions opposite of the cliff's edge. It was there that we separated. I watched for a long time as you had set off on your new path. Then I turned and set off alone. How we came to this cliff is another story for another time. This one is for the discovery of a new path to an unknown destination.

A new journey begins.

THE STORY OF THE BEACH

The path was rocky and steep heading down to the beach. Many times, I looked around to see if maybe you were following or stopped fearing to move forward and further away from where we parted. Maybe if I climbed back up you might be there waiting, and we could journey forward together. But there was no path leading back up to the cliff's edge, only forward to the beach. The sandy beach opened wide with pebbles, shells, and washed up broken things at the water's edge. The water led out as far as I could see. An ominous unknown. Dark clouds and storms collected on one horizon and clear skies and calm waters to the other.

I wander for what seems like days, picking up pieces of broken shells of our past. The beach stretched for miles, and in time I knew it was empty to me. There was nothing here that could grow or sustain me. Only by leaving the safety of the shore could I find the possibility of a new future, and the journey would be an adventure.

The Journey of Thom Slade

THE STORY OF THE BEACH – A journey from the cliff of divorce down to the beach of decision.

I can tell you the exact moment my divorce became final. Not because I popped the cork off a bottle of champagne or balloons fell from the sky but because the pain of the finality that cut so deep. I hate losing. In my marriage it felt like I had failed, and I was a failure.

I had just returned from a business trip and the first message I received as I exited the plane was from my lawyer. He had just left court and all the papers were signed. I was officially divorced. You would think from the year of hell I had just been through that I would have been happy. But instead, I started to cry. On the drive home I had to pull over, sobbing with a strange sense of loss, not victory or freedom. I just remember the finality of it all. The End. It took me some time to realize that this was not the end but the beginning of something new.

Heading down from the cliff and away from my past, the path to the beach was steep and strewn with heavy boulders. In an almost zombielike state, I made my way feeling half alive and numb at how my life had so quickly changed. As I picked my way down, I stepped further away from what I thought was to be. Away from family vacations, Christmases that I had known for 17 years, away from a future I had taken for granted. Each step seemed heavier than the last, the weight coming from the fear of something new–of being alone.

The beach was flat and wide, with white sand for as far as I could see in every direction. The waves gently stroked the shore, and it was a place of peace that I felt I could stay a while. And I did stay for a while, contemplating the past that was lost. Walking up and down.

But for all its peace, the beach was too quiet, too still, and there was nothing there to build on or grow from. Standing at the ocean edge, I could glimpse distant storms, islands, other places. And I started to wonder what these places looked like. What new thing might be there? I started to think about a new journey. I could not go back. That was gone. The only way was forward, out, and beyond. And then I came upon my way to salvation on the beach. A boat–something new and a way to expand my journey.

What's Your Heading?

A Time to Start and Choose

Like it or not, you have started a new journey, one where there is no going back, even if you're Elizabeth Taylor. So, glass half full, it's time to plan forward.

Looking at Shells

I wandered back and forth on that beach for what seemed like months. The only footprints were my own. I was scared of leaving "the known," so I continued to pace, looking for ways back to the safety of my marriage. As I think about those footprints, I'm reminded of how many times I looked for other footprints to follow, but I only found mine which returned to the same questions – Was it a mistake? Should I wait longer? Will she come back? Have I wasted 17 years? As I walked the beach, I found no answers no matter how many steps I took or shells of memories I collected.

I can build all the sandcastles I want, but in the end they all wash away. I have to move on with my life. The beach is beautiful, but I can't stay here.

I'm no sailor. This is crazy.

I like the analogy of a boat heading out to the deep open seas as we know what happens when a boat lacks a captain, map, rudder, or sails. The boat is tossed to and fro, carried at whim by the uncontrollable currents. It can end up floating aimlessly in the middle of nowhere, wrecked on rocks or left stranded on a deserted island. Unless the goal is to spend the rest of your life with a spherical lover called "Wilson," you need to plan where you want to go and define your new life goals.

Goal Setting

This is where the positive part of my changing life became apparent. As a couple, we made decisions together. We did things as a couple. Out of necessity of time and our joint goals, we probably had less time for some of our individual passions or hobbies. All this is as it should be in a long-term relationship. But now, I'm solo, the boss of my time and paycheck, the captain of my ship, the master of my plan... (OK I'm over selling it... But glass half full dictates.) You can decide what you want to accomplish.

Keep it simple. I spent the first year following my divorce just doing things I thought were fun. Not solving world hunger (which I probably should have) but instead my own. Eating out, enjoying solo my love of movies, joining stuff from indoor soccer (included hanging out with my friends, and beer, meeting new people, and laughing a lot) to Fantasy Football (included hanging out with my friends, beer, meeting new people, and laughing a lot…. and losing a lot more…). I took writing classes, spent a ton of time hanging with my kids, and created a list of 10 life goals which I wrote down on a giant pad. I can't stress enough how important it is to write them down and revisit them often. Remind yourself where, what, and why you want to accomplish. It is OK to be selfish and have fun! The key is the action. It helped, focusing on something positive separate from my present pain and the difficulties of living with my divorce.

Heading Out in the Right Direction

Once you have a plan, it's time to set sail.

Leaving the Stuff Behind

Your goals are not set in stone, nor should they be changed with your socks and undies (which should be often post-divorce). You may change your course, heading, and goals with your new life experiences while continuing to throw negative baggage overboard. What are the things you are holding on to? What emotional cargo is slowing you down? A slash and burn strategy of the past may not be healthy in the long run, so take time, quit cutting up pictures, and stay the course. Sail forward with more of what makes you happy and moves you towards your goals.

Look to the horizon. It is not the end of the world. You won't fall off, but you can find something new.

"Each journey is different, but many have traveled the paths."

The Journey of M. T. Lisle

How the hell did I get here?

I stand, frozen in this spot. My hands tingle. My feet cemented to the ground. My body feels hollow, like I'm not in it. I feel like someone just slapped me in the face, and I'm stunned, blinking over and over to make this place come into focus so I can see it. Understand it. Understand how I ended up here when I did everything to *not* end up here.

Ok, so I am human, and that means I did plenty of things to end up here, and I had a lot of help.

How did we get here?

The day it really hit me that my marriage was over actually occurred about four months after my divorce was final. I'd been doing the On My Own thing for nearly two years out in the open and a whole lot longer than that in secret. A piece of paper didn't feel like it changed anything--the piece of paper protected me and my kids. The piece of paper didn't feel like an end--it felt like relief. It felt like guaranteed peace. It felt like safety.

We got there because we didn't do what we promised. We got there because we didn't know how to care for and protect each other when life threw us punches no one should ever have to take--certainly not alone. And my marriage felt like I was always alone. And that's because I was. I know the person I married wanted to be the person I wanted to spend my life with--he just wasn't, and he wasn't honest with himself about that very important fact, so he couldn't have been honest with me about it.

The person you married never really existed.

I will never forget the moment I heard him say those words to me. And I'll never forget how the reality of those words made everything else make sense.

In the many months that followed, I tried everything. I'll go to counseling. He could go to counseling. We could go to counseling. We could redefine our marriage and make it work. We could start over where we were, forget the years before, and build a new "us" that would work. I asked what he wanted. I asked what he needed. I asked what he didn't need. And then I crammed myself into the shell that embodied that version of me, and it wasn't enough. I was the only one working at it, and no human can outwork a person who isn't trying.

So, we decided it was over and pretty amicably untangled our adult lives from each other as much as possible and as much as you can when you have kids. Have you ever seen an image of a tumor that has woven itself so deeply into someone's organs that it's impossible to separate? Or that the operation involved would cause so much damage to the original organs and tissue that they wouldn't likely survive? That's how I felt. It wasn't that I couldn't separate myself from him; it's that I couldn't imagine how to separate myself from Us. And Us was very different from Him.

Living separately from Us left me wondering who I was. In disbelief I put one foot in front of the other because life goes on and kids have to eat meals and go to school and feel loved and still go to everything just like before, but I felt like an imposter in what had been my life. *Us* no longer existed, so who was I now?

More importantly, who was I going to be?

Before I could tackle the future, I had to understand the past. Sifting through the wreckage could help me understand my part in what went wrong, what went right, and learn everything, everything, everything, I could from this mess of a life I found myself living.

I wanted to come out of this stronger and healthier, wiser and more hopeful because love is bigger than heartbreak. I just knew it.

It had to be.

Dear Self,

With Love, XXX

Views from the beach

A postcard to self of three positive things

My Self

C/O The Journey

What I learned from the Rd.

A Place, Startville

USA

OPEN LETTER

FRANCE LA POSTE

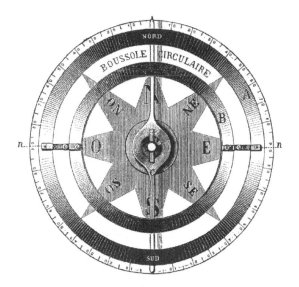

CHOOSE YOUR HEADING

You realize the time has come to leave the beach.

If you choose to contemplate what's ahead,
anticipating the rough waters, go to page 95.

Feeling Numb? Lay anchor at Numb Island page 35.

Or stay on the path and follow our journey.
Read on.

HEADING OUT & DIVING DEEP

After hauling the heavy anchor of your past on board, it would be easy to rest your tired arms, sunning on the gently lapping water, but your sails wave wildly in the wind and your boat slowly heads into deeper darker water. The smell of salt in the wind, the wild snapping of the sail, and the darkening depths beneath make you take the rudder firmly in both hands. You tighten your sail and with determination head towards your future. You can head anywhere, be free, but for the moment, your mind is drawn to the ever-deepening depths beneath you, the mysteries they hide, and the nervous fear of heading into the unknown.

.

After divorce or separation, life can feel like you're heading out to sea--to the unknown--tossed and turned by uncontrollable forces.

Heading Out

Depending on your level of anger at being "in" a divorce, you'll either hop, skip, and jump into the boat or be thrown in like a sack of potatoes. Either way you're in it with the anchor up, wind in your sails, drawn out into the very large uncharted seas.

And holy moly is it scary.

Yes it's big. I mean it's the ocean... but what's more scary is that I have the sailing experience of a cat named Mr. Nibbles who has lived indoors his entire life, wears little jumpers and seasonal hats.

Needless to say, I was stepping out of my comfort zone, and it was terrifying. One wrong move may not equate with walking the plank, but it could've been my house--or worse--my kids.

Leaving the Known to the (Fear of the) Unknown

First day at a new school, first date, trying out for football/play/anything, interviewing for new job, starting new job, anything that starts with "new" generally leaves me with a stomach knot and certain fear of failure. I'm sure anyone reading has experienced it. Neil Armstrong's "one small step" was probably prefaced by a small gas release in his space suit... Trying new things and stepping outside your comfort zone is, well, uncomfortable. I am a creature of habit who loves adventure, most usually when "adventure" is the only path. Once traveled, I will wear it out before being forced onto the next. On each new path I learned something, like a tree sprouting a new limb, and growing toward more sunshine and becoming more "tree" shaped. Stepping out to do difficult "new" things is worth every step of fear.

"If you don't try, you'll never know, and if you don't go, you will never have been."

I did not want to ever, ever in a million years of Hagen Daz ice-cream want to go through a divorce. But here I am, a survivor who has not only journeyed though it but expanded my horizons, learned a lot about myself, others, and the world around me. I've also come out in my opinion... and my mum's...which count) a better person.

That "one small step" was worth the scary million-mile journey.

Deep Water & Being Out of Your Depth

I have a healthy fear of deep water because I know I am guaranteed death by shark attack. Ever since I skillfully whined my way into seeing *Jaws* at the age of six, I have had a fear of deep water. (I was meant to see *Dumbo* and probably would have become the next Jacques Cousteau if my mum hadn't given in.) The 1 in 11.5 million chance of being attacked by a shark should set me at ease, but it doesn't. It is the mixture of the "duh-duh" music in my head and the unseen. It is also how I felt when the papers had been filed and the lawyers, family, friends, and ex started circling. I was out of my depth in the unknown.

The (Known) Unknown –

The odds of getting attacked and killed by a shark are 1 in 3,748,067. In a lifetime, you are more likely to die from fireworks (1 in 340,733), lightning (1 in 79,746), drowning (1 in 1,134), a car accident (1 in 84), stroke (1 in 24), or heart disease (1 in 5). *(ref i)*

I'm guessing the divorce death rate is probably less likely than the shark, so even though it has as many teeth and you still need a bigger boat, chances are with high likelihood that you will survive this part of your journey.

Time for a Deep Dive

It's fun to paddle and splash around in shallow water, but to move on you have to go deep. We can all see the trash floating on the surface, but what about the hidden sunken wrecks of past behaviors and relationships? On the start of my journey I found it was very important to spend time alone contemplating "The Deep." Not the metaphysical or mysteries of the universe but simple contemplation to look at me, my issues, failures, and successes to decide what was staying on board and what was to be jettisoned.

Diving deep is not to be taken lightly. I think all the years of toxic, wasted relationships probably created one ugly looking mother of a fish down there in the deep. I don't think at those depths it's possible to go out and slay the creature or send it deeper into the fathoms. But it is good to politely say, "How do you do?" recognizing your creation then moving forward reminding self not to create such pollution in the future. That is the crux of setting off on a new adventure in your life--coming to terms with the past, defining what those really were, and using those experiences no matter the beast to move forward positively.

Things You Can't Control

1.   **The Environment** - With both periods of calm and storms in finances, work, and life.

2.   **Negative People** - The toxic waste is out there. Choose where to swim.

3.   **Your Ex** - Is on their own journey, and you are not the captain or even the cabin boy/girl.

Things You Can Control

1.   **Speed** - Take your time, find yourself and your passions, especially before another relationship.

2.   **Heading & Direction** - Take the high road and stay away from the swamps.

3.   **Destination** - Where you want to go and how you get there is up to you and the attitude you take.

Sail safe at your speed and in a direction always navigating toward your destination.

Heading Out & Diving Deep

Twenty-something years ago, I bought the greatest pair of heather gray sweatpants.

They were perfect for the grocery store, road trips, yoga class, nearly everything! Think the LBD of uber casual--they fit great, feel super comfy, and are almost always appropriate lounge attire. I bought them at The Limited for $29.95 with a little matching zip-up hoodie (additional $29.95), and resembled a diminutive boxer wearing the whole getup. I remember wondering if this was an impulse buy and a shopping move I'd regret if I didn't wear it enough to justify the purchase. I bought it anyway.

My single-gal weeknight ritual went something like this: kick off heels, hang up work clothes, throw on perfect gray sweatpants, pour conservatively sized glass of wine, and read or watch Ally McBeal because who didn't love that dancing baby?

So I still have them...and they look like they have been through a war.

Each year I clean out drawers, making my obligatory Goodwill pile, and guess what I found in the shorts drawer? Yep, little gray sweatpants! I thought, "I don't really wear them anymore unless I'm the only one at home because those suckers are obscene!" The waist elastic emerges through a 3-inch hole on one side, there's paint all over the rear end from 15 different projects, and I made them into shorts at some point, which was admittedly a bad move but made sense at the time given the threadbare wear on the knees. Why in the world the sweatshorts were still taking up residence in my chest of drawers defied all logic. I've had them so long that they could walk around by themselves.

I tossed them in the Goodwill pile.

Then I took them out of the Goodwill pile and folded them neatly back into my drawer. Why? I just couldn't throw them away. After all, we've been through a lot together, the gray sweatpants with phantom legs and me. They waddled with me through two pregnancies until I traded them in for a pair of men's XL far inferior sweatpants. They climbed something like 37 collective flights of stairs moving into my first on-my-own apartment. Then the wearable security blanket moved into two more apartments and three houses. They downward-facing dogged with me in my first yoga class when I couldn't touch the floor. We got a new ACL, and the stretchy saviors actually fit over OR under the great bionic-looking knee brace without irritating my incisions. Their soft cotton absorbed a few tears when a separation and then a divorce became a reality, and I could get them dirty when I buried my daughter's cat in the yard and held her little shaking body while she said good-bye to her best furry friend. I'd forgotten until sitting down to write The Life and Times of the All-Knowing Sweatpants that I was wearing them when I got engaged and when I drove myself to deliver my first child at the hospital. (Another story for another time…)

The pants have traveled some serious mileage with me. My sidekicks. Like the clothing version of Tonto.

Now before the psychoanalysis begins, let me say that my attachment to the things isn't really all that complicated. They make me laugh. Those suckers would get me arrested if I sported them in the grocery store--they aren't even Wal-Mart appropriate! But they do remind me of how much I've grown up, softened over the years. The pants and I have lived a lot of life and have the rough places to show for it. At least I still have my legs, which is more than I can say for the pants. I can't really wear them anymore, but I giggle when I open their drawer and see them in there, tired from what I've put them through.

Why am I writing about an old pair of sweatpants? In all seriousness, I did some thinking about why I've kept something with no redeeming purpose. I landed on just because they remind me of what life was like at 22, my wide-eyed view of the world, and the many adventures I've traveled since. They remind me of the conquests, defeats, dreams, failures, and do-overs that led to new challenges. For some reason I can't explain, those beat up britches make me feel proud.

So I'm keeping them. How a pair of pitiful pants that would live a more productive life as a dust rag encourages me defies any level of reason, but they just do. I look at those hideous things and I see a Wonder Woman cape because I know with utter certainty that I will survive whatever comes my way, that difficult situations provide opportunities to grow, and that I'm stronger than Ally McBeal and that dancing baby ever dreamed.

I think it would be beyond weird if I framed the pants, so they can stay in my drawer. #pantspower

When I opened my at-the-time husband's laptop to get a jump on Cyber Monday, I somehow got lost in the settings and found some information that would forever change my life. Yes, I was wearing the sweatpants. My mind circled, swirling with questions and explanations designed to stay in the outer rings of the whirlpool, giving him the benefit of the doubt. There had to be an explanation, right? But the more I looked for a reason to pardon what I found, the more clear the truth of the situation became, and I found myself in the center of the swirling water, going under with no hope of being pulled out.

There was no way to ignore the truth of the facts and no sugar-coating that we were not who I thought we were.

Had things always been perfect? Of course not. Had we both made mistakes and hurt each other in the years before? Definitely. But several years earlier, we had hit the brakes and made a life-long commitment to each other that from then on, we would leave all of our past sins there, forgive each other, choose love and our family, or die trying.

I felt like I was dying in that moment, like the world would never be the same place, and I had no place now to fit in it.

Those next few roller coaster months are a blur I struggle to remember now, but I know medium didn't exist--I lived in a constant internal state of larger than life hope and a digging on the bottom with a spoon level of despair.

I did a few things right.

The day after the reality of my world tilted in the kaleidoscope of life, I called a counselor I trusted and made a phone appointment for the next hour she had free in her counseling schedule. At the end of that appointment, I scheduled one per week for the next two months because I knew one thing with certainty--my sweatpants weren't getting me through this. I needed a qualified, professional coach who would dig into this with me dedicated to the healthiest outcome for me and my kids. It couldn't be a person who told me what to do but could guide me in making my own informed decisions rooted in truth, reality, and a positive outlook for the future, whatever that entailed.

That was one of the best decisions I ever made.

When my family thought I had lost my mind or well-meaning friends told me it wasn't that bad, or bad enough, I could consider my decisions and actions with clarity in one hand and a solid understanding of healthiness in the other. People who loved us intervened with the best intentions, but they were invested in an outcome they could live with, not one that was healthy or helpful for my kids, my husband, or me.

In time, those close to me observed behavior and decisions that clarified for them my situation. In doing the intense work on myself up front, taking the right steps at the right time made it possible to avoid additional hurt for everyone. We avoided unnecessary fighting, excessive negotiating, and could more easily make short and longer-term decisions based on priorities (like our kids) than from a place of hurtful reaction.

I realize this makes it sound like an unfeeling walk in the park. Rest assured, the sweatpants and I curled up in a sobbing heap of grief, despair, anger, and self-pity on a fairly regular basis. When I found myself alone, at night when I'd hear a sound and couldn't sleep, when I would take the kids places and people we knew would smile awkwardly or ask horribly insensitive, invasive questions.

My mood could swing from determined and strong to angry viper then collapse into an emotional hot mess in the form of a human mop on my closet floor. It was terrible, but at the end of that, I was left with choices. I could define what actions I took next, who I wanted to be in this beyond difficult chapter of my life, and how I wanted to walk forward in what was a lot of life left to live.

The next year I focused on the kind of parent I wanted and needed to be to support my young children. The balance of caring for them and keeping myself in check involved planning lunches a few times a month with people I could trust to influence me in the direction I wanted to go, heading to yoga at least twice a week, and doing one thing each day to check in with myself on a soul level. This time carved out daily to take inventory of my intentions, my anger or sadness, my actions and choices, and how I viewed my role in my life kept me on track. I'm not saying I carried this out with any kind of finesse. Some days my insides felt black and cold. Some days I walked through my life like a gorilla on ice skates. What mattered is that I did my best to show up every day, own my part of things, and chose to be the best version of myself possible for one day. OK, sometimes it was more like one hour, but the point is that my mindset became a purposeful habit in thinking.

Over time, rebuilding my ability to trust people completely challenged my instincts. To say I have a hard time trusting people would be laughable! Trusting people lands up there with walking across the Grand Canyon on a tightrope...in very high winds without a pole. I want to trust people, build deep relationships, but it is extremely hard and feels vulnerable on a naked turtle level. Like zero shell at all. I remind myself that even if someone shows me they are not trustworthy, I probably will still survive. The size of my fear of being harmed in this way ranks up there with sporting a meat dress in a lion's den. The sad part is that people hurt people because we *are* people and we are really good at making mistakes, usually without intention. So, I continue to work on reminding myself that even when people make mistakes resulting in an injury that feels like a breach of trust, that intention matters. It also matters that they didn't hurt me purposefully. And sometimes people hurt others with excellent intent and precision. That's when spinning on my heel and walking away without another thought is easy. Keeping my feet glued in relationships where I don't know where I stand takes something out of me.

And this is my thing to own on my journey of recovering from the experiences that led to my divorce. It is still hard, and I more than long for the day that it's different. Trusting someone to be close and truly know me still feels like I'm a naked turtle at times, but more often these days, I'm comfortable without my shell. And those are the best, most precious moments. The world feels righted. Hope blooms in me. I glow with a settled resilience I haven't experienced as a naked turtle before.

I live days like these more frequently than I ever have, and I am so grateful for them. I also know I still have some work to do to completely eradicate the doubt that lingers, to allow the people who love me to be human too, and manage my expectations of their awareness of their actions on my lingering fears. Most times, I just say, "Hey, I need a hug." And the world opens up, presenting herself as a place safe to explore.

Post Card

THIS SIDE FOR CORRESPONDENCE

Dear Self,

With Love, XXX

Diving out Deep

THIS SIDE FOR ADDRESS

A postcard to self of three positive things

My Self

C/O The Journey

What I learned from the Rd.

A Place, Startville

USA

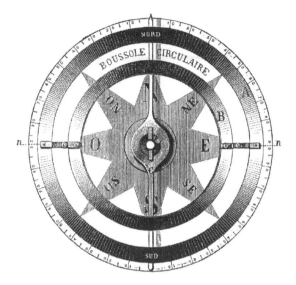

CHOOSE YOUR HEADING

Congratulations! You've survived the depths and are ready to explore new lands along the journey.

Have kids and lost your heading? Look for Steady Sailing page 62.

For introspection page 12 - Heading Out and Diving Deep.

Or stay on the path and follow our journey. Read on.

A CHEERFUL VISIT TO THE DESERT ISLAND OF LONELINESS AND DESPAIR

Days turn into weeks, weeks into months since leaving the shores and the one you thought would travel with you on this journey for life. But they are on their own separate course now, and you are alone. You have friends and family, but your bed seems very empty. Your day somehow less full. Your mind returns to past shores that no longer exist, and an island appears in the darkness with a tall lighthouse. Like a fly drawn to the light, you circle and land on the Island of Loneliness and Despair.

Why in the hell would you visit this place on your journey?

This stop is not a matter of choice or necessity, but for most, including me, you just have to stop there. Trust me, it is not one for the postcards. This place is a barren desert. Nothing new will grow here. It's hot as hell, and you seem to walk in circles muttering "woe is me," feeling like the fly, continually circling and banging your head against the light. The mythical answers you're searching for as to the *why* will not be found here, only a spiral of depression and angst. But you will visit.

Why am I here?

No, not the *big* question but one more for investigating why you cannot move on from your past. The pain of loss and loneliness hurts. It keeps you awake at night, holds you in your bed in the morning, and follows you around all day at work. And repeats. For days. And sometimes months.

I have memories of getting stuck in the shower. I'd sit on the floor, and just feel alone and sad until my chest hurt. It sucked.

Dying of Thirst Surrounded by Water

The weird thing about loneliness is that in a population of 7,714,576,923 (but who's counting) we are surrounded by people. In the shower, not so much, but step outside and you have your family, friends, coworkers, and even that topknot guy at Starbucks who says hello.

Desert is another word for beach!

Okay, maybe that is not technically true, but you get my gist. You must get up and go outside. You must surround yourself with positive people in positive situations. I'm not talking group hugs at the nude beach or telling Mr. Topknot about your life issues, your ex who left you, and your sob story. He probably also has one. It is just about connecting with others and shifting your focus from the negatives of **what happened** to the positives that **can happen**.

Heading Back Out to Sea

Only **you** can make the conscious decision to leave loneliness and despair. (As a note, depression is a real thing and you may also need to seek professional help.) That may be as simple as joining a club, church, or social venue to meet new people or making a point to schedule regularly hanging out with old friends at a book club, sports event, or anything. Meeting for a social beer is also great but be careful not to use it as an excuse to numb and blubber your tears into your best friend's ear. This just results in staying longer in the desert. Instead head back out on your journey and adventure to your new positive and exciting future.

Desolate. Quiet. Too quiet. One miserable emotional ghost town where nothing good takes place except getting the hell out of there.

The Isle of Despair.

I hate that place and still at times I fall into the trap door vortex that lands me smack dab in the middle of lifesucksandiamtotallytakingmyballandgoinghomefollowedbypoutywalk.

Then I get real with myself.

And I crawl into a ball with my hands over my eyes and sob. Shameless wailing that feels like no grief I've ever encountered in any other situation I'd consider grieve-able.

A dear friend of mine recently lost the love of her life to a terminal illness. This was a second marriage, a beautiful and much-deserved second chance for the both of them. One evening as we walked our usual route with canine children talking about the thing's girlfriends discuss on ponderous walks, she said something that quite frankly shocked me. "Divorce is worse than this, than losing someone you love too soon. I mean, this sucks but it hurts in a far less destructive way. He didn't choose to go. It's so much more horrible when someone chooses Not You."

Mrs. Not You right here, and I have to agree.

There are a million little fractures in my heart from my

divorce. A million first things on my own. Those awkward events where the blank space next to me felt so obviously vacant. Trying to fix things, the empty half of the closet, the stupid crystal picture frame he had to have on our registry, giving back the ring I'd worn for nearly 11 years-- the ring without an end that was to symbolize Forever, his birthday, our anniversary, driving past our first apartment, burning the garlic bread and remembering how he nearly started a fire in the oven the first time he tried to make me dinner by setting the garlic bread on fire, when friends tell you they saw him at dinner with someone, remembering my daughter's face when we told her Daddy was not going to live with us any more, when he moved in with someone else way too soon, when the house feels much larger and far too quiet because it's a Saturday night and the kids are with him this weekend.

Despair waits patiently for the raw edge to show and then rips into the spaces it finds a foothold. Even though it ended--and we have in so many positive ways mended our hearts and lives, knitted them carefully into something new and different, stronger and better--it wasn't always all bad. Despair knows that and takes full advantage when the chink in our armor finds itself exposed.

I think I cover my eyes and roll up in a ball when I cry because in some way I'm hiding from the things I don't want to see, from the things that wield the most devastating blows.

Am I too much? Am I not enough? Did I try too hard? Should I have tried harder? Am I even lovable? Will it always be this way? How long do I have to feel this way?

Sound familiar? My guess is probably. I'm also willing to bet those of us who identify with muddling through the desperate pain of rejection believe the lie that we are alone in experiencing this sickeningly awful loss.

Usually once I've let myself feel the unfairness of it all, I just feel better, like I faced the thing under the bed and figured out it wasn't a big scary monster dead set on eating me and repurposing my rib as a toothpick. Once I dump out the mess and take inventory or just feel it, I find out it's just not as crippling as I feared. I know better than to believe those things and shut them down as quickly as I'm able. Fear and doubt camp out, whispering to me when I'm tired, overworked, or my soul's undernourished, and the lie finds a way to seep into the old wounds. While its relentless pursuit festers, and I ignore it and keep burning the candle. With a blowtorch. Once I just let it out, I'm left with Garfield eyes and an excuse to eat a pint of ice cream. On my way to the bottom armed with only a spoon, I think about what's good in my life, where the quality lies in the day-to-day actions I take, and in the long game because that's what matters.

Things go bump in the night, and that's scary when I'm alone and I don't want to be. But now I know I can handle the bumps, that I'm equipped to care for myself and those I choose to support and love, who love me in return. I've learned to fix things or throw down the wrench before I make it worse and phone a friend.

The path off the Island of Despair is different for everyone who lands there, but all who survive have chosen to leave it behind.

Resilience
Truth
Promise
Hope

Let the Light in. Open the curtains wide and feel the sunshine, the source of life for all of the beautiful things that grow and nourish us. It's just cold and one long miserable rainstorm when residing in despair. There's nothing helpful that comes from staying to roll around in the muddiness of a past that, well, just left you all dirty. A visit back to the desperation of how that time felt only provides two benefits in my opinion (and benefits might be a bit of a stretch). Visiting reminds me how much I don't want to be there and serves as a healthy deterrent to finding myself there again for any measurable length of time. Looking back at that place, that time in my life, and remembering how it tore me apart brings my current reality--my presence in the present--into sharp focus. Like a kaleidoscope in my hands, the slightest twist in perspective reveals a different picture worth examination.

Despair provides me with a benchmark, a point of reference for how far I've come, how much I've grown, and my heart swells to near bursting with gratitude and thankfulness for the quaint, quirky village that is my wonderful hodgepodge of a life I've built, a place I never would've ventured had it not been for the less than preferential experience of divorce. Headed for whatever adventure awaits, I don't even look back once I'm away from that place. And I smile because I can't quite remember why I found it so dreadful and scary in the first place.

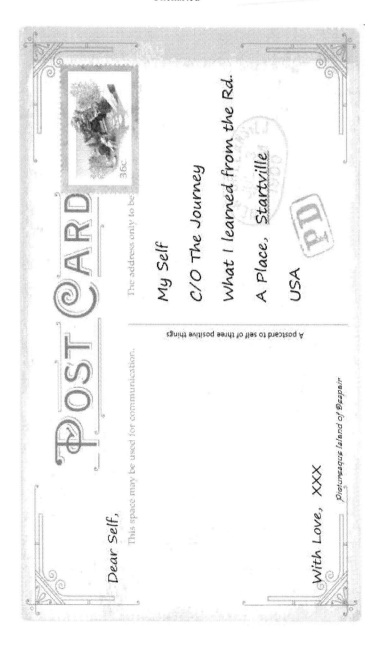

POST CARD

The address only to be

This space may be used for communication.

A postcard to self of three positive things

My Self

C/O The Journey

What I learned from the Rd.

A Place, Startville

USA

Dear Self,

With Love, XXX

Picturesque Island of Despair

CHOOSE YOUR HEADING

You've escaped the clutches of the Island of Despair

Now on to Adventures on the High Seas Page 71.

Or stay on the path and follow our journey.
Read on.

LAYING ANCHOR AT NUMB ISLAND

The storm rages and the ship's timbers and mast creak and crackle. The violent howl of the wind is all I hear as the saltwater blinds. Out in the middle of those skyscraper waves that feel like body blows, one after another, I pray for a safe harbor, for my senses to block out the storm that rages all around and in an instant, I arrive at the still and silent shores of Numb Island.

The sea can be a terrifying expanse where at any moment sudden storms can tear down your mast and your ability to move forward. Snapping your rudder to leave you without direction, the powerful and terrifying expanse sends you crawling into your bunk to pull the sheets over your head and block out the world.

Numb Island is a real place. Many go for short visits throughout life and some, unfortunately, never leave. The fear of present or future pain and loss that is out of our control can drive us to simply ignore the facts or events that surround us. We block out reality and numb our senses, especially in the beginning of a divorce storm. The unknown buffeting can become just too much to handle.

What's the Draw?

At some point, everyone wants to block out negative or scary parts of their lives. And I mean everyone. You might be Mr. or Mrs. Perfect and not venture as deep or as long inland, but we all visit Numb Island. It could be a death in the family, an issue at work, a breakup or divorce, but short-term escape from reality can be a place to catch your breath or collect your thoughts.

I probably have spent too many nights on Numb Island. I should not use excuses, but I will.

Divorce kicked my confident ass. Things I thought I controlled, I didn't. Things I believed about myself, my character, my family were wrong. There were days when I woke up and collapsed in the shower and just sat there. I felt very alone and not in control. There were weekends when I numbed. It could be as simple as my favorite suspension of disbelief, going to the movies, hiding in the dark from the world while I watched others battle right and wrong, win and lose, live and die. Outside I had to go back into the real world with real people needing real answers. I loved escaping to the movies. Then there is alcohol, especially beer, which I love. I have to be very careful as the son of an alcoholic. Definitely during the year of my divorce and following I used the excuse to party too hard, drink too much, and think too little. I have thought many times about how easy it would be to float off and stay numb. Drugs have never been my thing, and luckily, I hate hangovers more than the night that caused them. It is tempting to continue to hide from pain and just float on, oblivious, uncaring, and without worry, but only for a little while.

My greatest fear during my divorce was losing my children. The thought of seeing them only every other weekend almost broke me, and the separation reality of week on, week off, drove me to numb.

I am not saying the court was wrong, or who should or should not have won as I'm sure my ex experienced the same feeling of loss from the other side of court.

Divorce is hard. Reality is harder.

I have also experienced, seen, and spoken to dozens of others that go numb in their workplace. They literally wake up years later after going through the motions, getting the job done, but not being part or growing in their career. Don't get me wrong. Money and stability are good things. I'm not suggesting in the spirit of *Eat, Pray, Love* that we gallivant around the world cooking, drinking, and sleeping with strangely accented people. (I'm not selling the negative virtues of doing this as well.) The reality of real responsibilities keeps us doing what we are doing until we are ready to move on emotionally.

Why Stay?

Alcohol, sexual addiction, drugs, or anything used to numb-out the world does not have any long-term benefit. For the moment, you may feel empowered, as though you are moving forward when in fact, you're not moving anywhere you want to end up. We cannot build a strong foundation on Numb Island. In the end, after a moment, a few days, weeks, months, or even years we have to go back into the world and move on with the reality of a new life.

For some it can feel impossible to leave, and the only way may be to seek professional help. I escaped because of the needs of my three kids and the everyday chores of school and feeding them. It became my saving grace. Filling that hole with more of their love and being more involved helped raise my anchor and escape the Island of Numb. Also, the desire to try and create new things in my work life and in new relationships helped put wind in my sails. Leaving does not mean I don't return occasionally, when the world gets too much, and I need a movie.

Three Tips to Make Your Trips Short or Escape Numb Island

1. **Reality Bites** – No matter how numb to the world you become, it's always there waiting for your return. Your temporary escape is just that. Pain of love lost will lessen but the issues and memories around it still need to be faced. You cannot avoid reality. Sounds dumb but understanding helps you move on.

2. **Positive People** – Hanging around with negative people doing negative things to avoid their own realities, will not lead to anything new or positive. If your influences are negative, change them and your environment as much as possible.

3. **Positive Goals and Aspirations** – Look forward, not just on the past the current storm. Have plans and set goals for personal growth.

Beware. Sometimes the numbing wind drives me to neighboring islands of Self-pity, or the dangerously attractive and fun Wild Oats Island. More to come on those adventures.

Checking Out

The work of divorce demands nearly my full attention. If it's not trying to remember all of the responsibilities of making our day-to-day life happen, it's the constant reminders that life as I knew it—as I expected it to be—doesn't exist in my world anymore.

It's walking into the closet, forgetting it's half-empty now. It's running into old acquaintances at the store who ask where he is, how he's doing. It's going to work without my wedding rind when everyone notices, and no one says anything. It's deciding what to do about our Christmas card this year—just send a picture of the kids?

It's the first birthdays, parent teacher conference, performance, meeting—everywhere requires a brave face, and I can't do it one more day because the world holds up a mirror with a reflection so painful that I can't stand feeling any more.

When pain gets the better of us, its human nature hardwired in our reptilian brain, to avoid it. Our sense of self-preservation screams at us to run. Avoid further injury. Give up the fight in order to survive another day.

In that place, I feel defeated, completely beaten, and I can't take one more blow. I am decidedly throwing in the towel, returning, broken to my corner where there's no one who can adequately patch me up.

When pain feels like this, every lie ever whispered in my ear volunteers a quiet reminder that I am in this place alone. Defeated.

Finding any way to peace seems like a better option, a do-able alternative to this misery.

Numb Island, it's the place we go when we can't deal with our reality. We check out. We can't even be angry because that means we still have the energy to fight. Numbing takes all kinds of forms, none of them particularly healthy because we are sitting on the bench of our life while the war is still happening on the field. We ignore the slaughter, pretending it will all be fine like hiding my eyes in the scary part of a horror movie. If I don't see it, it's not really there. I'll just ignore the screams. (I seriously hate scary movies!)

My version of numbing meant holing up someplace alone and dreaming of fairy tales that were never going to materialize. I occupied myself with one project after another, requiring all of my free time and making it nearly impossible to notice the painful realities I couldn't face. My involvement took me away from dealing with relationships I didn't have the energy to manage or repair. It kept me from diving into issues that needed my attention, that I didn't feel equipped to handle or even know where to start. My brand of numbing is isolation, a walled-off barricade impenetrable to anyone who might either inflict additional harm or remind me of the parts of my life that seem too overwhelming to manage on my own.

Numb Island floats in a hazy sea of fear, masking the horizon so we are too terrified to venture back into the waters of real life. When I don't know what I'm up against, I don't know how to proceed, and I believe the lie that I am supposed to know everything.

When I don't know how to feel, how to react, how to mot make it worse, I numb by checking out. And my relationships suffer immensely for it. I suffer immensely for it because isolation never healed anyone's heart or rebuilt their life.

I remember looking at my kids and wondering why they weren't telling me stories about their day, and I quickly realized it was because they knew I wasn't listening. I wasn't there.

On Numb Island, you're always that last one to know. I didn't notice I was wasting away in dangerous territory and desperately needed a way out. A light. A path. An answer. I had plenty of reasons, and two of the most important reasons were scooting their dinner around on their plates but not really eating it.

The way out of the lethargy of numbness lies on the same path that brought me there. Unfortunately, to heal from pain, I had to walk back through it. Facing up to the big hairy scary things meant approaching them with honesty and transparency. I didn't have to have all of the answers, but I did need to acknowledge those aspects of my life that puzzled me and find some helpful tools to work them out.

The way back, still riddled with rocks and uneven ground, seemed less scary for a handful of reasons. At the other end of this part of my journey stood a healthier, more capable version of me, hand in hand with my kids, deserving of a mom who was present in their lives to notice the small things. Acknowledging my inability to save my world and my fear of failing when I tried turned out to be the simplest part of the answer—admitting that I could not fix it, that I could not fix all of the broken things in my former life. When I shook hands with that truth, I could leave it behind and focus on getting back in the game because my team needed me.

While I couldn't fix our broken past, I could get back in the boat, steering toward something more productive like building something new that felt like a future. With each swish of the oar through the black water of unknowns, my fear faded because I left them behind and focused on the aspects of my life I could rebuild. That looked like taking the time to listen and providing encouragement. It meant stopping to be grateful because I had so much to appreciate. It looked like laughing at my failures and being OK with do-overs.

When I leave this isolated place, I realize I'm also grateful for what I learned from spending some time there. Regardless of how devastated I was after the reality of the end of my marriage started to set in, I realized that it didn't have to take me out at the knees. Taking a break to gain my bearings and get a glimpse of who I did not want to become propelled me forward to build better relationships, to appreciate the little things, and look forward with anticipation tow hat's next.

Post Card

for correspondence

for address only

Dear Self,

With Love, XXX

Numb Island Sends Her Regards

A postcard to self of three positive things

My Self

C/O The Journey

What I learned from the Rd.

A Place, Startville

USA

NEW YO
15 1933

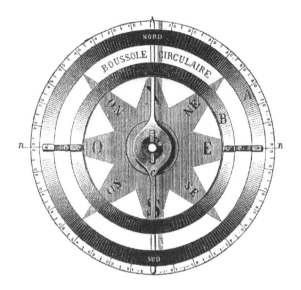

CHOOSE YOUR HEADING

The blood returns to your fingers and the aches leave
your bones as you flee Numb Island, refreshed and ready
to take on the World.

Search for lost treasure but beware of pirates' page
83.

Need to slow the adventure and focus on your young
cabin crew look to Steady Sailing page 62.

Or stay on the path and follow our journey.
Read on.

THE DRAW OF WILD OATS ISLAND

Wild Oats Island is not hard to find. It always seems to be there, glowing like a neon sign on the horizon. During hurricanes and calm waters, always there, a tempting island full of mystery and the excitement of the unknown. It draws travelers from near and far with promises of passion and the numbing of pain from lost love. Its beaches are beautiful, and its entertainment world class. Why not stay forever? Because it's a short-term distraction from reality. A place that some never leave but also never move on to find new growth and real-life adventure. At some point, the suntan lotion wears off, and you start to burn. The numbness clears to reveal a very lonely hangover. Beware of Wild Oats Island.

One of my weirder post-divorce experiences involved the number of "congratulations" I received from male friends and work colleagues. It was weird and also depressing. I know they were trying to bring excitement and cheer to my newfound singledom, but the majority were still married and could only see the divorce as a freedom to return to some kind of 80's fraternity life full of one-night stands and wild parties. For a long time, I questioned their motives to see me on the wild side. Were they so unhappy or bored in their own relationships that they wanted to live vicariously through my exploits? Or was that the "guy" thing to say and they just thought I needed to move on to another relationship, get married, and get back in their couples' fold? Either way, I found the best way was to walk the line and learn from both sides of the fence.

A Walk on the Wild Side

Like a racehorse chomping at the bit, I found a number of friends–both male and female–at the finalization or even as the key changed on the door were off to the one-night races. Like a starving person suddenly being introduced to a buffet, many found singleness to the dating world. I can only explain the appeal of one-night stands as validation that they were still attractive and desirable. That somehow, in many cases, even though their life partner cheated, the leaver was the idiot for leaving such a sexually attractive "young" machine. As with travels to Numb Island, sex is a great way not to think about what happened and where you want to go past the *Now*.

I'm not here to bullshit you on this journey. I am no saint. In the years following my divorce I have made many mistakes, but many also were not. New relationships post-divorce are full of pitfalls from the past and are part of growing on this journey. I moved on from feeling like I was cheating on my ex on a first date to comparing and competing with others, to real relationships that frankly were deeper than my 17 years of marriage. That was not anyone's fault. I am learning to love myself and others differently.

And you will also meet the crazies who expect you to meet them at their car on the first date, get on a knee and put their shoes on, kinda sexy, kinda embarrassing, but funny in hindsight, from the ones who don't want to eat but order a $100 dinner and talk about themselves for three hours, to the ones with deathly fears of fruits and their shapes cannot be in the same room as them to the ones that you have to squint hard to make them look like their profile picture, and the other dog lady, cat lady, the one that sent me a picture of her blow-drying her wet hair because she was late? and all the blind date dog masseuse that used to be a stripper… All an adventure and all not coming back for a cup of tea.

My message from my journey is not to hide from Wild Oats Island but watch your time there. When you go, understand what it means.

Sex, Drugs, Rock, and Regret

"If you're going to kick authority in the teeth, you might as well use both feet." -Keith Richards

A hangover can take a couple of days to recover. Some things, a tad bit longer…

If your last dating pictures came from a Polaroid, it's important to know about this little thing called social media that even your mum and maybe especially your mum as well as all your work colleges like to investigate and print the evidence on t-shirts. If you have kids, you have been preaching about keeping things off the web that would make their grandparents or priest blush for years. But the rule of thumb, unless you're Keith Richards, keep the memories to yourself and try not to share with the world. Note to guys, no one really wants to see that *special* picture.

And the gift that keeps on giving, not STD's but STB's. I have a divorced acquaintance who was gifted a baby from his one-night stand as he finished out his forties without the mother. His free singledom came to a swift end. (It's a beautiful baby, and they are very happy, just maybe breathing in those early days may have been less stressful and he might have showed up with more hair in his kids' graduation pictures.)

Also consider why you went and what you were looking for. It's usually something more to do with yourself than another person. Learn to ask the why and move on as a *whole* person and not one looking for someone to plug your hole and stop you from sinking.

Time Served, Lessons Learned

"It was the best of times, it was the worst of times, it was the age of wisdom, it was the age of foolishness." -Charles Dickens

Pretty much sums it up. But if there are pearls, I learned from my visits and also from those of my friends, it is to never squander time. Use every moment, experience, and tear to move towards your goal. If it is to find your soul partner… well then plan for it. Learn from what you liked and what you didn't and create a plan to find your perfect mate. Know that you might not find your rock star in a choir or your violinist in a mosh pit.

Write a letter to your future self and partner

- Describe yourself
- Your passions
- Things that make you different
- List your life goals
- Your loves and hates, hard yes's and no's, and deal killers (I'm a no Disney character tattoo guy…)
- Describe what you are looking for in a partner in detail using the above as well as how they look, what they value, how they will treat you and what you see your future together looking like.

Print it. Keep it. Feel free to update it. But what you might settle on stature, don't settle on character.

Stupid Mistakes and Other Horrible Decisions

At some point, in the raw months after the ink dried on the divorce papers, well-meaning people suggested that I start thinking about getting back out there, finding someone new, or maybe some hobbies where I'd undoubtedly meet people.

As one of the minority in the post-divorce days I think, I had zero interest in dating, relationshipping of any kind that might mess with my heart or carefully balanced life I'd been working so diligently to keep as normal as possible for my kids. I felt the need to assert my OK-ness, but not by going on a Divorce-cation to Vegas, having my boobs put back where they started before two kids, or going generally crazy. It's just not my style.

I self-destruct much more internally and in a go-big-or-go-home kind of way.

In this case, I think taking a look at why matters. Family has always felt like this delicate, precious way of being eternally connected to people in a way that defies any undoing. Like a forcefield of the purest, strongest kind of love. I watched people who had this my whole life, wanting it for myself. When I was small, I don't think I could articulate what I felt was missing that I observed in moms and dads and their children, but I certainly admired it.

I never planned to get married. I always saw my life as one never-ending adventure, living somewhere like New York City or Paris, and loving my work, whatever it was, as I knew it would include something artistic or creative. Clearly that didn't quite happen.

All this to say, being the parent who was left to protect the *familyness* that remained--my sweet son, my bigger than life daughter, and me--became my entire reason for breathing from morning until night and kept me awake the rest of the time. So, partying like a Rockstar then coming home to our *home*, where I was working so hard to provide solid footing for the family I had left just didn't sound like anything other than epic stupidity.

I'd been through enough.

And survived.

And worked too damn hard to keep it together to wreck my hard work and, more importantly, my kids.

For a year, my kids stayed at home every night. On the weekends their dad had custody, they came home at 9pm, slept in their own beds, and woke up in them the next morning when their dad would pick them up and have them back by 2pm on Sunday. The positive side? My kids' lives felt stable to them. They missed their dad, but he would see them during the week, and it didn't seem all that different to them.

Of course, this couldn't last forever.

For one, I was exhausted. I also never really had any adult things to do. I spent time with my mom almost every weekend. One or two nights when the kids were with their dad, I'd go to yoga, grab myself dinner, and eat at home while watching a movie. That lasted about a year, then everything changed.

My ex (and his girlfriend) decided our arrangement wasn't working for him (or her), so whatever wasn't nailed down in our decree went out the window. The results were these: we had to move, I had to pay for private school without his help, and my kids would now be staying with him overnight on his weekends. This shattered my carefully guarded little fortress of safety and isolation.

And it was the best thing that could have happened to me.

At some point, an old friend introduced me to another friend who had lost his wife to cancer about five years before. By now I'd been on my own for three years give or take, so getting out of the house for more than work, volunteering at the kids' activities, and standing Saturday night dinner with my mom seemed like something worth consideration.

So, I went on practice dates with no strings attached. Dating with training wheels, one might say. This included dinner and movies and sometimes coffee. That ended when he was set up on a blind lunch date and felt like it was not the right thing to do where I was concerned. I deeply appreciated that a gentleman considered how his actions might affect my feelings. And then I lost my movie partner.

I never really did the go crazy off the deep end thing. I've typically made most decisions in my life around not becoming a walking cliché, so that mindset probably saved me some heartache.

Getting Real

Now, in the spirit of the topic, I may not have been to Vegas until this last year, but I did once go out with an old friend from high school who said this when dropping me off later than either of us originally planned. "There are some stories we will never tell, and that is one of them."

Honestly, it wasn't terrible but did involve one impulsive cannonball contest into a swimming pool. No harm. No foul.

In walking through this past decade of my life, most of the heartache I've endured resulted from my trusting people I shouldn't have and wanting to believe the best when the evidence didn't add up. Sometimes we want to be loved more than we want to admit that what feels like love, or the hope that it could be, really isn't.

After all, divorce annihilated my deepest trust, left a gaping wound, and a pain so completely encompassing I never thought it would stop.

That place is dangerous because in time anyone enduring that level of pain without relief from it will go to dangerous lengths to feel anything that isn't pain. My saving grace was a larger fear--that I absolutely could not destroy our life. So, I didn't do things that I thought would bring anything dangerous near us. And I honestly didn't have the desire to do anything along those lines. Hashtag Boring.

A few years ago, I met a treasure of a person who fell head over heels for me in a big hurry. I kept waiting for the other shoe to drop--he had to be married or a con artist, maybe he was some kind of secret axe murderer? He was none of those things. He was a total catch of a human being, who happened to have three kids younger than mine and lived 6 hours away. After not long enough, he started talking about moving here to be closer to me, but his kids would have to stay where they were. This is more complicated than it sounds because his kids lived less than a mile away in a less than positive situation and needed to know they could hop on their bikes and be at his house in minutes. If he wasn't there, I didn't believe they would be safe. So that ended because kids have to come first, and I was losing sleep at night over three sweet children I'd known a few months. I just knew it was the right thing. And it really was.

All this to say, the lull away from the pain is a lethal temptress. People blow up their lives and make terrible choices because it stops the pain now. That same temptress doesn't mention that drowning the immediate pain in something disingenuous only compounds the pain when the euphoria wears off.

After-school specials about drugs and kidnapping effectively impressed upon me that drugs would definitely kill me and probably so would creepy men offering puppies in ice cream vans. I stay away from those things, but I am just as guilty when it comes to avoiding my own pain. I isolate myself because I erroneously believe that there isn't anyone who will sit in my pain with me and shine the flashlight on other things. The people who could provide that were just missing. I had those people and then we moved away from them. Relationships like that take time to build and grow. They last but they are different when those people are far away, and all of my people were far away living their lives and managing from one day to the next. It's just hard to keep up with people in the same way when we don't see each other as often. And, let's face it, when we talk, it's catch up and talk about what's been going on in everyone's lives. I don't think it's necessarily cool to call someone up and grieve at them.

So, I don't.

After we moved, we started working on making couple friends. Couple friends, especially younger ones, don't know how to respond to people with marriages that are breaking. They responded more like we had something they could catch, like the flu but more deadly. So, I lost the few people who were here. Over time, I found new people, and at times I honestly think I found people who might not have been the most positive influences, but they were people who generally showed up for me, and I could show up for them.

These days, I have different people whom I love. I love them because they have lived life with me. We have been through some tough times and been present for each other, spent time together just because, and just lived life. That's how relationships are grown. They grow when I invest myself in them

The Stupid Mistakes

Every stupid mistake I've made started with the best intentions.

Two deep desires drive the way I pursue things: the desire to matter to people and situations I care about and a relentless commitment to this odd sense of rightness for every human being, the etiology of which I can't identify. It's like a superpower but way less cool. I can't shake it-- instead I take up for the little guy, help people who need it, and fight for the underdog. Believe it or not, this is not always the popular thing to do. Once I understood this about myself, I realized how I fell into a few situations that weren't good for me, and unfortunately there wasn't a Me around to say, "Um, you're stupid and hurting yourself to help someone else who really doesn't care about your best interests."

I reconnected with an old friend who invited me to meet for lunch as we had just lost touch over the years. So, lunch ended up being drinks after work when this old friend came to town. While it was fun to catch up, in hindsight, I should've just left it with, "It was great to see you, and I'm so glad you're doing well," and put him on my Christmas card list. Instead drinks turned into dinner and easy conversation about what we were up to these days. Then, out of the blue, he said, "Why didn't we end up together?"

I answered, "Because we probably weren't supposed to."

It just ended up not feeling right. When divorce shattered my heart, it also did a number on how I saw myself as a partner in a relationship. For lots of reasons, I believed I was not lovable. I hated it, but I still believed it. Here was a person I'd known since I was a teenager, telling me I hadn't changed a bit, and that basically I was lovable.

What are the lessons learned?

I felt like a person who was permanently flawed. Here was a person telling me otherwise, speaking specifically in opposition of the most painful injury I'd ever sustained, the one wound that kept opening up. This wasn't the solution.

When someone told me exactly what I wanted to hear, I desperately wanted to believe it.

When that person wasn't entirely honest about their

availability or willingness to step into my life, the potential for disaster and even more personal devastation was imminent. Putting myself in that situation was a stupid mistake. An innocent, well-intentioned one, but still not in my best interest. A quick and graceful exit was in order.

Recovering from divorce involves diligent, hard work on oneself. It wore me out, and that's a given. The temptation to engage in the temporary provides a reprieve from facing scary things that cause hurt. Considering the fallout doesn't usually enter the equation when offered (fill in the blank), but whatever is filling in the blank will most likely just increase the size of the blank. Going crazy and making impulsive decisions provides a short-term distraction and compounds long-term heartbreak and inner conflict. I was hurt enough, so hurting more didn't sound appealing.

Other Horrible Decisions

I know I'm in the minority here, but I think online dating isn't the greatest idea. Apparently not all dating sites are created equally but hooking up with random people just will not land anyone in a better spot. It's highly more likely to result in a plethora of problems.

In my experience, my horrible decisions included trusting people who weren't trustworthy, so I decided trusting people in general was not on my list of things to do. It got me nowhere but hurt there for a little while, so I took my little ball of trust and hid that thing at home.

During that season of my life, I think I put off a vibe that radiated something along the lines of "If you touch me inappropriately or pull some other piece of meat action at me, you'd better be out of reach because you may not survive with all original appendages."

A group of my friends attended a concert one spring evening. The rare occasion I went out with them had occurred, and we found a spot in the back where we could see the stage. This idiot decided an appropriate way to flirt with me included sticking his boot up the back of my skirt. And not a little bit. I turned slowly and glared right at him. Then I turned back around and took a dramatically large step away from him. Most folks would get the message. Not Cowboy Einstein. He did it again, and I turned around and let him have it. Then I left. I didn't feel safe in a place where a man could act this way in front of a large number of people, and not one person said a thing. It completely ruined my night. Honestly, I was terrified. I got to my car as quickly as possible and drove home. Pulse racing, I got home, locked myself in and got to bed with my heart thumping. I was scared.

In the end, I'd not been harmed, but the fear of being in a place surrounded by people I knew and enduring a threatening situation probably served me well. When my Spidey-sense kicks in, I remove myself from potentially dangerous situations. Was I in danger? Probably not. Did I really want to stick around and find out? Not a chance.

In my ten years of figuring out how to be a single gal again, I've probably missed out on some fun and played it more than safe. My approach may sound unappealing and probably contributes to my current single status, but I am comfortable and proud of my example and priorities. Everyone has to define those boundaries of comfort, risk, and safety for themselves.

THIS SPACE FOR WRITING MESSAGES

Dear Self,

With Love, XXX

TOLEDO OH
DEC 20
11 – PM

TOLEDO, OH
DEC 20
11 – PM
O

1910

A postcard to self of three positive things

Post Card

FOR ADDRESS ONLY

My Self

C/O The Journey

What I learned from the Rd.

A Place, Startville

USA

"What Happens on Wild Oat Island, Never Stays on Wild Oat Island"

USA 36¢

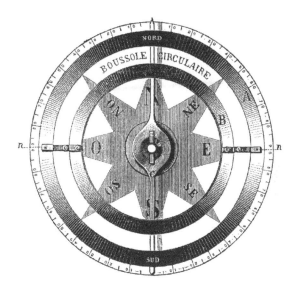

CHOOSE YOUR HEADING

Lessons learned it is time to move on.

Feeling the pain of regret and remorse from sowing your Wild Oats? Head to page 26.

Seeking More adventure? Head out to the High Seas page 71.

Or stay on the path and follow our journey. Read on.

STEADY SAILING WITH KIDS

Storms come and go, but you never leave the rudder. Your hands are blistered, and your skin burns from the sun by day and the storm's stinging seawater by night. But you must move forward, ever forward, holding the course. Holding your craft straight on its journey as the world tries to batter and toss you to other distant shores. You hold tight and pray for strength to finish the journey, reach your destination, and safely deliver your precious young cargo to the calm waters and distant shore that you want for their future.

Steady as She Goes

If there is one thing that I hope you take away from this book, it is knowing that above all things your kids come first during and after your divorce. (If you have them... otherwise it's your cat or your ex's 401k and American Airlines points.) "Putting a brave face on it" may seem fake, but your positive optimism and clear sense of family direction will help them through and beyond this difficult life transition. They know you are in pain and that life as they know it is changing. They did not make the decision to set out on this journey. They are your most precious cargo and, for both theirs and your own sake, you need to make it as calm and consistent as possible. The opposite can come back as a teen hurricane or even extra lodgers in their late 20's, 30's, 40's and beyond.

A Consistent Course

We all know there is not a plan during the divorce other than to win. But to win what? Unless you are divorcing a Donald, there is no positive financial gain.

If you find yourself mid divorce, I'm sure you are on an emotional rollercoaster. I know I was. There were many days that I could not seem to keep it together nor could I tell you one iota of what my life plan was. But I kept it away from my kids and in the confidence of a few close friends. In elementary school your child may have issues with little Jonnie pulling pigtails. By high school it's sexting, constant emotional drama, raging hormones, and homework. Keeping your home as a place of calm with consistent messaging on being positive about life, its opportunities, and looking forward will keep your kids coming home and save some of your hair left in your head.

Keep it simple. Post school schedules and all activities on the fridge. Make reminder notes and enforce family dinners together WITH the phones (including yours) switched off. Simple to say, difficult to do. It's ok to have some TV dinners. It's ok that they spend time alone in their rooms. Just keep it together. Keep in contact with your kids' friends' parents, teachers, coaches, and the ex, even if only via text or an app.

Being consistent is not to be confused with being strict or iron-fisted when parenting. It means consistently communicating, listening, and reacting with logic and not emotion to difficult situations. There will be storms and lightning as your kids transition from home to home and as they get older. Know what fight tis worth fighting and what is just being stubborn. To me, parenting is about getting my child ready to set sail on their own as confident and independent captains of their ships rather than passively going through life as tethered lifeboats, constantly bumping my rear and pulling them along on my journey.

Lead by Example

During the times that you don't know what to do, act like you do.

When it's dark, be a light.

How you act, what you model during the toughest and sometimes darkest times of your life, and how you treat your ex during those times will shape your kids for the rest of their lives. So, steady as she goes. Breathe first before speaking. Think long term and not in the moment. Be as even-keeled as humanly possible.

I try to model the "fruits of the spirit." Nope, it's not something I drink, though that could be an adaptation that works. I try to model actions and produce the positive characteristics in my life that I want others to see--loving more, being joyful or finding happiness during tough times, being at peace in my current situation or place in life, showing more patience, being good, kind, gentle, humble to others and myself, and show positive self-restraint in areas that could cause harm to others.

The Ex Factor

Simply never, ever, ever, eeeeeevvvvver (or as much as humanly possible) say a negative, harmful, disparaging, or hurtful word against your ex in front of your children. Keeping consistency is part of keeping respect as a parent and the role of being a parent. If you slip up, apologize quickly and make sure your kids understand that it is not an acceptable behavior. On bad days, a soundproofed car or with closed eyes in your special place in your head, feel free to swear it off. Or take it out at the gym...

Becoming The World's Best Sailor

A goal of your new journey should be to become the very best You, and with that, the very best parent. Finish your journey bearing bountiful fruit with awesome whole kids.

But the fruit of the Spirit is love, joy, peace, forbearance, kindness, goodness, faithfulness, gentleness and self-control. Against such things there is no law.

Galatians 5:22-23 New International Version (NIV)

The Single-Parenting Perspective: The Case for Keeping Kids' Lives Consistent

"She's a teenager--she'll get over it."

Actual stellar advice spoken aloud to my mom when my parents separated.

Besides the obvious uncaring nature of the insensitive comment, it's completely false. No shortage of research about children supports the integral importance of parental stability in the life of children. Parenting is not for the faint of heart or those without a solid level of commitment. Children don't get to choose their parents. They don't get much of a say in large part about their growing up at all-- their livelihood is up to their parents.

When the little pink lines materialized in the diminutive window and I realized I was going to become a parent (ready or not), everything changed for me. Every decision, every single one, my kids became a factor because if I was going to do this parent thing, I was going to do it with everything I could throw at it.

My parenting resolve probably kept my marriage together much longer than it would have if we hadn't had kids. While I'm not proud of that, it's the truth. So much of my marriage was completely entangled in building and protecting, loving and supporting my family. MY family. So when it was obvious that my marriage would now have to become a completely separate thing from my family, I knew like it was a fact in my skin and running through my veins, that my children would need me to step up in a completely different way.

I remember deciding I would do everything I could so my kids wouldn't feel like they were missing out because they had parents who were divorced. Absolutely not going to happen. That means I've often been the only mom on Boy Scout campouts, there are really no "weekends off," and I've learned about video games, superheroes, slimy stuff--you get the idea. One year, I came pretty close to coaching a boys' basketball team! I just refused the idea that my kids would miss out because of decisions outside of their control that would completely change their childhoods.

Above all else, this meant getting over whatever resentment I felt toward their dad. I had to find a way to put aside my loss and occasional desire to smack him and show up with my big girl pants to partner with him because I knew if I didn't, the effects on my children would quite literally scar them for life. It was already going to be hard for them. I chose not to make it any harder, regardless of what it cost me.

And it did.

The days they would come home from weekends with his girlfriends' kids and tell me about the exciting things they had done or the vacation they were going to take. I had to filter my personal feelings and respond in a way that supported them and building healthy relationships with their future step-siblings. I reminded myself on a fairly regular basis that the most positive outcome for my children included as many people in their corner who loved them as possible. Step-things included.

Over the years, it's also meant that at times, I have defended their dad. I have sided with him, and I've made it a priority to support him in being the best parent he can be. I can be a cape-wearing Supermom all day long, but there's one thing I can never be--their dad. A dear friend of mine pointed that out to me very early on, and I am so grateful that her words sunk in and have continued to resonate with me for a decade now. That hasn't always been the easiest way to carry on, but I remain convinced it's the most honorable avenue. Taking the high road proved the most supportive of my children in both the immediate and their futures.

I missed out on the opportunity to model a positive, loving, unshakable marriage partnership for them, and I grieve that most about my divorce. So maybe it's a consolation prize, but I purposefully model respect of their dad. I've modeled what two-parent support of children looks like every time we have shown up and sat together at parent-teacher conferences, gymnastics meets, awards ceremonies, performances, and birthdays. Whatever didn't work between their dad and me, we realize that we have these two miracles in common and that we are our best selves when we cheer them on together.

When my kids are adults, my greatest accomplishment as a mom won't appear in diplomas framed on their walls, the balances in their bank accounts, or relics of their accomplishments. It will show up in their character and their relationships, their ability to forgive, their caring for the people in their corner. Their confidence in themselves and in knowing what respect and commitment can look like will materialize in their adult lives--not because it will magically happen because life is not a fairy tale. But the happily ever after exists when kids see the benefit of respect and responsibility for those who are closest to them.

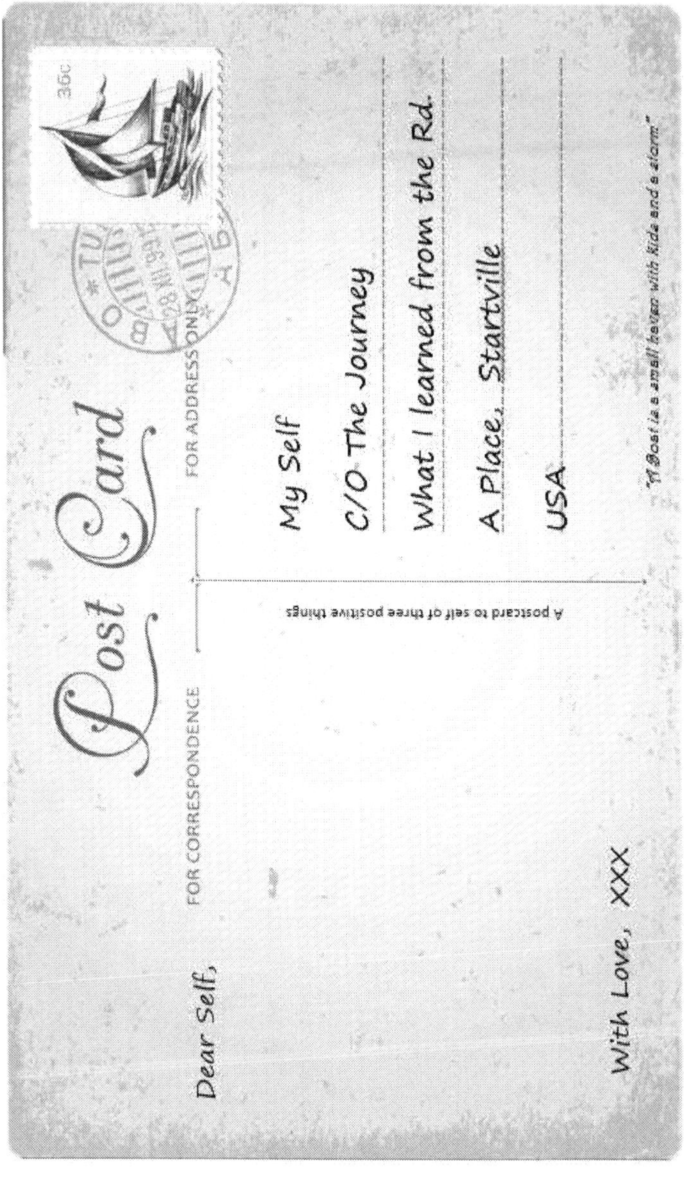

Post Card

FOR CORRESPONDENCE

FOR ADDRESS ONLY

36c

Dear Self,

With Love, XXX

A postcard to self of three positive things

My Self

C/O The Journey

What I learned from the Rd.

A Place, Startville

USA

"A Boat is a small helper with Ride and a storm"

CHOOSE YOUR HEADING

Kids are settled. Now it's "ME," time. Head over to
Self-Love Island page 105.

Still in the midst of it, learn to Ride Out a Storm.

Go to page 95.

Or stay on the path and follow our journey.
Read on.

ADVENTURES ON THE HIGH SEAS

"Avast ye Swabs..." or something like that you scream in a "piratey" voice to absolutely no one. Life aboard the HMS Rolling Solo is not so bad. You are the commander of your ship and platting your destiny. You can sail wherever you want (depending on the alimony you may pay or receive), whenever you want (depending on your kids, cats or job). Life on the high seas is full of adventure, except that you're new at this so you've run aground a few times, held the map upside down and almost sailed off the edge of the world, and maybe awakened the Kraken. Setting course to life's new destination ends up not being the straightest and maybe with a bit of pirating booty on the way.

Being Consistent

Post-divorce, things can get a little "normal." And in many cases, after is a highly stressful, emotional, drama-filled divorce and the turmoil of not knowing what is going to happen next never mind the future. Where you're going to live, child arrangements, and finance makes it seem impossible to focus past the "now." So, life on the high seas can seem slow and monotonous some days. The adrenaline is gone, and the days settle into a new normal of kids' homework, packed lunches, work, and laundry. During the "new normal," it can be easy to nod off course and steer towards the rocks.

Shipwreck Coast – Look for the Lighthouses, Not the Sirens

Boredom can also lead to the desire for companionship and the lure of the "sirens" on the rocks (I'm sure there are also male sirens… just google it). The same jagged coast that draws us also warns us with lighthouses. The opportunity to swipe right can just be too strong and lead to entering relationships before being ready. Instead take your time at sea, especially the first year, to build your relationships with your friends. Get involved in new activities to improve your well-being, meet new people, and make new friends with similar interests.

Look at it this way. You are a sexy, beautiful, smart dude(tte). Meeting someone is not going to be hard. Jumping into your next relationship will take away from your once in a lifetime "solo" voyage around the world. Yes, you could meet Mr. or Mrs. Right Siren and live happily ever after, but more likely you will end up on the rocks and not finish your adventure, never reaching your true destination. So, sail awhile. Listen to that terrible song by Christopher Cross, and sail, seek, learn, and grow.

Sea of Regret – Can go on forever. Get over it.

"The past is the past" but also "history repeats itself" can leave one in a bit of a conundrum. How far and for how long do you focus on the who's and why's of your divorce? Focusing backward constantly and consistently will lead you into a whirlpool of anger and sadness that is very hard to escape without becoming unbearably bitter. For me, the self-reflection worked more positively the further I got away from it. You need time for the wounds to heal, and constantly picking at them only leads to infection and slowing the healing process.

After reflecting, if there is one regret that I identify, it is the threat or use of the word "divorce" towards the end of my marriage. The "then why don't you leave" conversations open up Pandora's box in a marriage commitment. It becomes just a word, and every time the box is opened, the more the word grows into a natural thought and progression, like suggesting freedom, greener grass, or a "way out." All marriages have issues. For me and my future, I know better communication is key and a passive-aggressive use of words is a door to another failed relationship.

Pirates, Shark Infested Waters, and Sea Monsters

Your high seas adventures will be full of new exciting and sometimes scary experiences. He is some of the snares to keep an eye out for.

- **Pirates** – Someone always trying to steal your shit from the credit due at work to negative friends stealing your happy positive day. There is a reason they fly skull and crossbones… steer clear of bad people!

- **Sharks** – Just when you thought it was safe to go back in the dating pool. Take time and date yourself the first year, no matter how pretty the white teeth, they circle and bite!

- **Sea Monsters** are creatures from your past. Watch your words especially around your ex or you may awaken the Kraken!

- Lost in the **Bermuda Triangle** – Beware of hanging out in places with no stars to guide or wind for your sails. Vegas may be great for the weekend, but a week can take your treasure and ability to move forward.

- Stuck on Rinse & Repeat in **The Whirlpool from Hell** – Don't expect different results by doing the same negative things or hanging around with the same people. Get out there and try something new!

Course Correction = Navigate = Re-calibrate = Revise = Reset

I've lost the "stars" many times as I have journeyed, visited islands and oceans that were not on my course. I've learned and lost and lost and learned. You are your own captain and also first mate, cook, and engineer. You have the power to chart your course, set the pace, and reach your goal. Mistakes will be made, and off-map excursions will be explored. It is ok to forgive yourself, but you will not forgive yourself in the long run if you give up on your true journey, short-changing yourself in reaching your destination.

Mapping a Course with Positive Influences

I love being outdoors!

Take my phone, watch, and everything else with a plug and replace it with a trail map, my backpack, and set me loose in the mountains for a few days. That is my happy place. While backpacking opens access to beautiful places I'd never see otherwise and solitude, the potential dangers include a list of Things That Could Go Wrong.

- ✓ Bears.
- ✓ Weather changes.
- ✓ No water.
- ✓ Injury.
- ✓ Snakes.

Experienced backpackers plan for the what ifs and generally arm themselves with knowledge before landing in a tricky situation. I even pack a snake bite kit along with my water purifier, an emergency beacon, moleskin for blisters, dry socks, warm layers even if I don't think I'll need them. The Boy Scouts have it right--Always Be Prepared.

The Post-Divorce Minefield

Before my divorce was even filed, people volunteered their opinions on every topic from finance to parenting, dating and changing the locks. The unsolicited advice didn't align with the way I wanted to carry myself through what I was sure would be one of the most difficult experiences of my life. Some people truly believed they were being helpful and supportive, but in the end their negativity and encouragement of truly spiteful and in some cases reprehensible behavior became just one more thing I had to deal with and sucked energy away from more positive endeavors.

I learned to keep things to myself, to walk through my daily life operating as if, meaning I acted how I would behave if this situation was a simple walk in the park. When anyone brought up my soon-to-be ex-husband, I immediately shut down the conversation. People quickly learned that I was not going to listen to anything negative about him. After all, the injury wasn't theirs; it was mine. And I was going to manage it on my terms.

In the years following and now a decade later, I still work to avoid toxic situations and influences that don't align with the mindset I work to cultivate. I'm hesitant to label a person as toxic because I hope I give people the benefit of the doubt. Are they 100 percent toxic or are they making a decision or engaging in an action that brings toxicity to the situation? In all honesty, I probably give people too much rope here and have suffered from negative influencers in my quest to be fair.

Brittney Got It Right - Toxic People Are Dangerous

People who create the greatest success in their lives kick toxic people off the island and never even consider a life preserver as a consolation prize. Done. Moving on. Anyone or anything that pulls them away from their goals, consistently discourages the pursuit, or generally pulls down the morale of those headed in that direction simply isn't welcome.

I think there's a difference between a person who injects toxicity into my life and well-meaning friends who lovingly intervene out of genuine concern, pointing out what I'll call blind spots in my life. Sometimes it takes a friend to ask a hard question. Those people are important, and in my experience those people have earned the right to speak into my life because we have built a high level of trust over time.

But a toxic person negotiates situations and manipulates people to achieve chaos.

I've never understood this, and I'm grateful for that. I don't understand why anyone would purposefully cause any other person sadness, harm, pain, or discordance. I mean, life is hard enough!

I've run into my share of toxic people in my time. I'm not talking about someone who's in a rough patch or just having a bad day. You know the type--this is the person who consistently points out the downside, how any situation could potentially go wrong. They bad-mouth others and look for ways to create conflict. In my early single days, I had my fill of conflict, so inviting more unnecessarily seemed completely insane. When someone asked me if I was having a divorce party, I am pretty sure my mouth fell open because who does that? OK, if you're having a girls' weekend to get away after a divorce, that's one thing. An alcohol-induced frenzy involving a life-size pinata ex-husband look-a-like and a blow torch, not so much. In the end, what does that accomplish?

Know When to Hold Em, Know When to Fold Em, Know When to Walk Away, Know When to Run - Kenny Rogers

In the beginning, I worked hard to become the kind of single-parent and single person I could lock eyes within the morning when I approached the bathroom mirror. Aligning myself with like-minded people made that a lot easier. These days, I still keep the radar on when meeting new people, in a crowd, and within my relationships. I find that regardless of my intentions, I am absolutely influenced by the people I am around, so I invest my time connecting with those who challenge me to take positive risks in stretching myself, who have my very best interest at heart, and who are the kind of people I want to be like. Does this mean I keep a list, and if someone tips to the naughty side, I cut them out? Not at all, but it does mean that I am mindful of how much time I spend with them, and I am diligent about what topics might be off limits. With those guardrails in mind, my hope lies in growing my own confidence and leadership by modeling a healthier example. I'm not always successful, but I can't quite get to a place where I am comfortable with leaving people out or cutting them off, unless it's an extreme situation.

My litmus test for making hard decisions lands on communication. Adults should be able to have adult conversations with the end goal being ironing out miscommunication and looking for understanding of another's perspective, views, or needs. Sometimes I can't be what someone else wants me to be. Other times I don't want to be what someone else wants me to be. Sometimes I wasn't aware of what someone else needed or wanted from me. With gentle but productive conversations where the goal is to understand and learn, 99% of the time everyone leaves feeling like they have a better handle on what's going on and what isn't. I'm not bothered by difficult conversations because I'm typically a better-informed person on the other side of them. I generally feel less confused and more at peace because the conflict or rough spot is smoothed out or at least I know I gave it my best shot. If a person can't have a hard conversation, listen or contribute to finding a solution, or sees this as a fight to be won, that's a very clear message to me that I need to take a large step back and rethink my investment in this relationship.

This happened not too long ago with a friend who was kind of in and out of my life for a handful of years. Some strange behavior that didn't add up over time led me to reach out just to have a conversation in my effort to understand where this person was coming from. I reached out and asked her to meet me for coffee. No response. I called and left a message asking if she had a minute to talk. No response. I left it for a few days then called again and said I really needed to just talk with her and asked her to please call me when she could, that it was important to me, and I assured her that I just wanted to get her take on a situation.

After a week, she called me back. And right out of the gate, it was an attack. She was angry before I'd said a word. I hadn't made accusations. I hadn't even told her what I wanted to discuss or understand. She knew. My guess from the reaction was that she knew she was in the wrong. I never got more than a few words in edgewise before she yelled the emphatic suggestion that I visit a fiery place with lots of brimstone…. In the end, this wasn't a relationship I could salvage, not for a lack of trying on my part but because it's impossible to have a healthy relationship with someone who isn't capable of engaging in a productive conversation over seemingly little things.

Recalibrating: Tread Lightly But Carry a Big Stick

When I head out to spend a few days in the woods, I plan ahead. I plan for what I hope to experience--peace, solitude, taking in the beauty of the experience and the views--and also for the potential challenges like running low on water, raccoons getting into the food supply, an unforeseen change in the weather, and a potentially dangerous emergency. I emulate the same walking through the winding path that is life, hoping for breathtaking vistas but treading carefully because I remember that I am in the wild where all living things are doing their best to survive their circumstances. Bears don't really want to kill people. They are generally protecting their cubs from perceived dangers. They might be hungry, and I look like a snack. People who aren't living as their versions of themselves operate in much the same way.

POSTKARTE

36c

My Self

C/O The Journey

What I learned from the Rd.

A Place, Startville

USA

A postcard to self of three positive things

Dear Self,

With Love, XXX

Adventures from the High Seas – The Postkar Sends her Regards

CHOOSE YOUR HEADING

You've traveled the High Seas and seen the World,
but now it is time to Dive Deep and discover what is
underneath page 62.

Still traveling? Watch out for the storm.

Go to page 95.

Or stay on the path and follow our journey.
Read on.

PIRATE'S BOOTY - PROMISE OF TREASURE AND PITFALLS OF DEBT

A few weeks turn into months at sea. No sight of land. The water and, more importantly, the beer has run dry. Food is almost gone, my cat looks more like a juicy roast turkey every day, and yes again, we are out of beer. The further from shore, the more desperate for "something" I become. The need to fill my days and help forget the past. Maybe "things" will help? New car, clothes, shoes, dining out, vacationing, home improvements, change of job, scenery, and meeting new people. But how to fund such exciting expeditions to new worlds and experiences? With a blink of an eye, there on the horizon, a ship with its flag waving invitingly—the Visa/MasterCard skull and crossbones...

The Promise of Pirate's Booty

Nope. This is not a post-Halloween/divorce dating story. It is much much scarier than that. It does involve the promise of treasure and short-term pleasure, but most of all the pitfalls of long-term debt.

Zero Percent Booty

My divorce was expensive. I mean I spent a shed load of money, and eight years later, I'm still paying. I wish I could have been more logical in my divorce spending. But passions run high in the divorce high seas and so does the desire for the most expensive legal representation possible. Did spending a ridiculous college tuition amount of money make a difference? I don't think so, but at the time I felt more secure and slept a little more soundly.

I lost financially but gained personally in my divorce. I lost a lot but gained a fortune from the relationships and experience with family and friends and as a person. If I had a boat that first year, my financial sails were made up of two small handkerchiefs. It was very slow moving at first. Frustratingly slow, but in hindsight my need for full speed ahead would have landed me on the rocks.

Numbing with Credit Happiness

Silence was my worst enemy and fear post-divorce. It's a weird feeling being in bed alone after a decade and not hearing another breathe (or other nocturnal noise which may have caused the divorce). The silence of the first weekend without my kids or pet was not only weird but terrifying as the permanence of it settled in. It is during these times I needed to numb my feelings with noise of new things and activities. Just getting out of the house helped. I could watch a movie or be happy alone as long as there was noise and activity around me. I have seen many get lost in these post-divorce distractions by going a little nuts for a while numbing the silence. Whatever the activity, funding is required. A family trip here, some home improvement, going out more, meeting new people, and dating definitely started to add up along with the alimony. Getting divorced is expensive, and being divorced is not initially an easy time to save.

Why is it the more debt you get in, the more pre-approved credit card applications you receive in your mailbox? I can recall receiving dozens every week, a card for every color of the rainbow all at zero percent interest for the time it takes to open the envelope. The key to managing these financial acrobatics lies in having a long-term plan with the opportunity for some fun and short-term sanity.

Gold Digging in Dating Minefields

Dating is expensive. Really Expensive. Not just the apps, but the dinner, coffee wining/whining and dining in the hunt for that rare diamond in a mountain of coal. Coal mining is dirty hard work… so before picking up the ax, decisions really should be made as to what you are looking for, where to go prospecting, and identify whether you really are ready for your next relationship.

Are your ready to date? What are you looking for and why? And can you afford it? The best investment is time spent on yourself. No, don't get all creepy, but seriously–date yourself. Spend the time finding out what makes you tick, reignite your passions, and go do them. Save some money digging up rocks by investing in yourself and the future diamond you will find.

Some Debt is Priceless

I have some very fiscally responsible friends who look at any type of debt as a stinking dead fish. Some debt I believe can be mounted as a trophy. Investing in debt that creates lasting memories are, to coin a phrase, priceless. Some of our best times were on ski trips and summer vacations that were credit-card funded. We needed to just get away. We used this time to bond as a family, laugh a lot, twist a few ankles, and get some amazing pictures. Also sometimes getting away from the problem helped me look at it in a new light and come back refreshed to start again. I am so thankful for a close friend letting me take my family (and mother-in-law) to their lake house the first summer of my separation. I was thankful for the long drive as the further away I drove, the closer together we grew as a family. It helped me stand back from the battle and realize there was no value in a long-term war. It was time to move on and be a positive influence for my kids and myself for the future. The gas on that trip wasn't cheap, but the long-term savings emotionally paid back tenfold.

Paying the Piper, the Ex and the Lawyer

The worst thing about debt is that you have to pay it back. The longer it takes, the more it costs. When making those payments, it is really easy to get a little (OK, a lot) sour. But bitching and moaning about it does not make it go away any faster. Instead I've found it just costs you more personally. Carry the blame flame too long and it will burn your fingers and your whole soul to a crisp. No matter how unfair (don't get me started...), give it up.

Don't let that sad point in your life carry on and define you to your new destination or you'll become the new Moaning Myrtle of Harry Potter fame, always complaining about the past that you cannot change (and hanging around the toilet U-bend all alone).

Losing the Debt Anchor and Sailing Free

It is hard to focus on the long term when halfway through the marathon, you ended up at the starting line. Frustrating as it is, it is what it is. You have to put your big boy/girl pants on and plan for your financial future.

Staying the course with long term plans and goals should be balanced with your current needs. Stick with your job until you know where and what you want. It is easy to understand not wanting any association with the past or wanting something different, but fast boats (and cars) have slow payments. And credit cards are the biggest sharks in the sea. Sail with caution.

Getting a Handle on Finances for Single Parents

In ten years of marriage, I never paid a single bill.

Prior to getting married, handling my finances included rolling out my tiny hanging file system, and writing actual paper checks for all expenses, folding them with accompanying stubs into an envelope, and posting them with an actual stamp. In the handful of years following college graduation, I'd paid off nearly all of my college loans, had no debt including my used Honda, and lived on my own in a trendy North Dallas apartment. I saved for any vacations and cooked at home during the week to save money for The Future.

So, the part of the here's what's mine and here's what's yours conversation with my soon-to-be ex went nothing like I'd planned.

I knew we'd opened college savings accounts for the kids when they were born and paid attention when we purchased two houses. I knew what we generally spent in a month, that we had life insurance policies in the event of a tragedy, and that we planned to drive our cars until the wheels fell off since cars are depreciating assets....

I knew nothing.

He handed me a file folder approximately the thickness of the Yellow Pages and said, "Here's your half of the debt."

Did he say debt?
What debt?
We have debt?
How?

My half was in my name and landed in the nether regions of five figures. Five encroaching on six.

If the impending divorce was the right hook, the financial blow was the upper cut that sent me to the floor of the ring with the referee counting.

The reality of my situation settled quickly. I knew I had two choices: freak out or find a solution. Freaking out promised to solve nothing, so I rallied the troops in a large hurry. I called two friends who knew a thing or two about finance and my mom. All gave me the same advice-- protect your credit, get a handle on spending and expenses, and pay off the highest interest first.

That's what I did.

Surveying the Damage

Before I could attack the problem, I needed to understand exactly what I was handed. I audited our expenses, looked at what I was spending on managing our home, and what expenses I could eliminate. I stopped shopping for myself completely. I had clothes and shoes and didn't need more. I looked at my utilities and shopped for lower rates for everything and made quick changes. I quit buying books and got a library card. We almost never ate out, except on special occasions or at restaurants where sharing made sense. (Think pizza...) I paid every bill the day it arrived, which meant I always knew where I was in terms of my monthly budget. And yes, I joined the banking future and opened online banking and savings accounts to pay my bills online. Within one month, I had a strict budget, a savings plan, and had decreased our monthly cost of living to a degree that would allow me to pay off all credit card debt in four years.

I did it in just over three.

In the process, I found that I entertained my kids in different ways. We didn't go to Chuck E Cheese, we packed picnic baskets and explored new places. We spent more time with extended family and helping them with tasks at their houses like raking leaves and planting flowers in their flower beds. We went camping and hiking on Spring Break instead of skiing. And in a few short years, our financial situation looked very different.

Rebuilding the Financial House

In this time, we also sold our house. I could not afford it on my own, so moving became imminent. We moved in with my mom for a few short months that ended up being some of the most fun times of their childhood. I read them all of the *Little House on the Prairie* books in three months every night before bed. (Grandma too) I also sold my truck because I needed the equity, and gas and insurance were killing me. I ended up leasing a gas-friendly car with a low insurance premium and low payment which ended up costing me less per month than Bertha the Gas Guzzler.

That spring, I worked with a realtor to find the perfect house. This friend understood my situation, knew my limitations, and also appreciated my goals for finding a home I could afford in a neighborhood suitable for raising kids. I looked at four homes and made an offer on what is now one of my proudest accomplishments. This investment radically changed my financial future and enabled me to check so many boxes. I invested in a place we could make a home in an area that embraced us in community with positive equity as the cherry on top.

Looking Ahead

These days, my financial question marks include thinking about retirement, sending my kids to college, and honestly making decisions about investing in our quality of life. I'm in a position to loosen the belt a bit so we go to lots of movies, shop a bit more, and completely splurge on ice cream, but I still keep a handle on spending and saving. I never want to be a financial burden on my children, so working with a financial planner helps me navigate making decisions about my financial future.

In the end, the life lessons learned forced me to grow up financially. Faced with financial disaster, I could walk the plank or take responsibility for my situation. Those times were challenging and scary. I lost lots of sleep worrying about days ahead and how I could manage them. What I discovered in the process of cleaning up the mess was that I could overcome seemingly insurmountable obstacles in areas where I had no real depth of knowledge.

Planning for an Army of One

Looking ahead, I wonder what my future looks like from time to time. Would it be easier if I shared my life with someone? Sure, probably. But I know better than to throw the chips to the wind, put it all on red, and hope for the best. If the day comes when I hitch my horse to someone else's wagon, I want to enter that chapter of my life as an asset and not a liability. More than one divorcee has looked to marry into a situation where they are "taken care of," but that doesn't sit right with me. I've learned too much and value what I bring to the table separate from my finances. I'm proud of my accomplishments and any wagon hitching will be to someone who values the same.

RÉPUBLIQUE FRANÇAISE

CARTE POSTALE

Correspondence

Dear Self,

With Love, XXX

"Searching for Pirate Booty, but Only Found Crabs"

V 01 - 123,456

A postcard to self of three positive things

36c

My Self

C/O The Journey

What I learned from the Rd.

A Place, Startville

USA

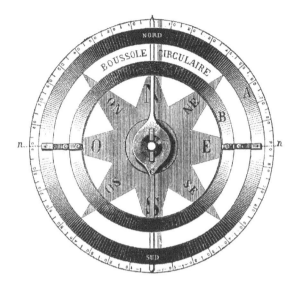

CHOOSE YOUR HEADING

With your newly found inner treasure stored, it's time to invest some of it back into your "self" page 105.

Not feeling it or anything? Head to Numb Island page 35.

Or stay on the path and follow our journey. Read on.

RIDING OUT A STORM

It has been weeks of beautiful calm sailing--the boat skimming across the water's surface by day and gently rocking at night with the peaceful lapping of the waves against the hull. It seems you have left the pain of your past on the shore far away. Life is restored. You are in control of your journey, and the forecast is clear, that is, until a dark storm appears out of nowhere. Your past crosses the horizon and quickly blocks the sun, the wind cracking and tearing against the sail, the rain stinging your eyes, and the waves tossing your boat. Each crash seems to make it shrink to the size of a child's toy, in what seems like the endless flash of lighting and roll of thunder. Where did the blue calm skies go and how will you ever survive this storm?

You've Weathered the Divorce Storm – Calm Waters Ahead?

The wave swells are crashing in. Each one feels like you're a little more swamped, a little more underwater, and to the point of sinking.

I know. As I have been there.

The safety that was my family home and a partner of many years seem miles away as I drift into uncharted water. There are days when I feel I'm cresting on the wave and can see the shoreline, only then to sink again in a sea of uncertainty between the waves that hide the safety of shore.

A divorce is not a life event for which anyone plans. In hindsight "divorce insurance" might have been a better investment than a pool.

A divorce can also very much seem like a hurricane that destroys relationships, family, and bank accounts. I have met many that believe that once the storm passes, they will be in the emotional clear skies. The truth is that the rumble of thunder, showers, downpours, hail, lightning, and occasional flooding will most probably continue with the growth of your kids and ex after college graduation. Maybe still into the occasional grandchild birthday, Christmas break, or limitless number of social gatherings until you reach that point and understand storms do pass, but there will be others.

You might let the dust on your divorce papers settle, before perfecting your Bumble/Match profile. It is really easy to think that plain sailing is ahead, that the ink is dry, and the past is, well in the past. But no matter how far from shore, there are bound to be difficulties with your interactions with the one who was once your "one."

No One Schedules a Hurricane

I live and annoy many around me with my "iiwwi" mantra. But it really changed me and how I weather the storms in my life. I was--and still am--a control freak in many parts of my life. Through my divorce, I have learned that no matter how I react to certain circumstances, some days the rain comes sideways. In the past I have carried frustration and anger for days at things I cannot control, namely other people, family, and my ex. It's in these times of heavy hail, that the only reaction that works is to not have a reaction. To understanding that some things are out of my control, and that "It is what it is" is the only way to tie yourself to the mast and ride it out. I don't mean throwing your hands up covering your ears and making a loud lalalalala noise as you run in circles and passively aggressively fight the storm, but instead understand that even those who accidentally or purposefully try to cause emotional harm are also hurt. Poking a tiger probably means losing a finger.

Holding the Course - Focusing On the Plan and Not the Pin

The safe course of action in an emotional storm? Always look back to the map and your plan of where your new chartered course is taking you.

Know that the storm never lasts forever. It feels like it might, but the waters will eventually calm, and you will see land again.

Look positively to the future and the storms that will come and go.

Benefits of a Storm

- **Washes away dirt & tears** –Storms remind us that we can start again with even the pollen causing our allergy headache being washed down the drain. Take the same opportunity to take stock and wash past anger away.

- **Feeds new growth** – Even the desert blooms with a little water. You might feel stuck, lost, or walking in circles. Take this time to water your life passions and creative talents. Read, write, draw, or get back to your favorite hobby (unless it's line dancing… I don't like line dancing…)

- **Signify a season change**   Time is the great healer. No matter how hard the downpour or how drenched you feel by life, you can also change yourself and your outlook. Storms will continue to come, so prepare yourself and your attitude to be ready to have fun and jump in some puddles. Watch your new garden of opportunities grow.

Sailing forward in full rain gear on the HMS iiwii.

Navigating the Rough Spots

You think you're OK and something comes up… How do you handle it?

Things you thought were settled are still there, and you thought they were done.

Rough patches are part of life for everyone.

In a healthy marriage, two people go through those experiences together. If one person has a rough day, the other shows up for their beloved, supports them however they need to be supported. If a financial hiccup happens, there's both another wage earner and someone to hash out the plan to recover. When one gets sick, the other can take over and let their partner in crime rest and recuperate. Kids have to be in two places on opposite sides of town at the same time? No problem! Divide and conquer.

Divorce changes this whole scenario. Rough patches present challenges, and they tend to come often when there's only one car, one income, one enforcer-doctor-cook-maid-et cetera. No sugar-coating it. It's just what it is, and sometimes that can be stressful. I am so used to being a one-woman show that this is my typical operational situation. I expect to be busy with my kids and getting all of the adult things done because it's my life. I find the bright side in the process of doing those things to a level some consider annoying, but it works for me and provides my kids with an adult model of responsibility and capability. Sometimes it annoys them too, but I believe they will thank me someday. (Or not, but they will be able to change lightbulbs, laugh at roadragers, and hopefully figure out a workable solution when they face a challenge.)

I also know when to call in the cavalry. I am not too proud to ask for help, advice, directions, or feedback, and I do it often. I fully realize that I will make mistakes, but I sincerely want to continually learn about myself, my shortcomings, and how I can make improvements.

Because the worst thing in the world to me is not trying.

I made the decision well before our divorce was final that I would have as positive a relationship as possible with the person I'd promised to stick with forever. We have two incredible kids deserving of our best efforts not only to parent them well but to work together in supporting them. That decision led to so much goodness in the lives of my kids. Birthdays are not awkward. Holidays are not dreaded occasions. And I believe that their graduations, weddings, and all the other milestones to come will follow suit because, of all the things we couldn't manage together, we are madly in love with our children. And we choose for things to be as easy as possible.

That's not to say it's all glitter and sunshine. We manage two different houses with completely different dynamics. Their dad remarried and added a step-mother and two step-children to their family. Here, it's just me and the dog. Sometimes we don't see things the same way or manage situations with identical perspectives. When those times come, the old frustrations volunteer and I am tempted to jump right in and rehash the past. Sometimes my frustration gets the best of me because I'm a human being, but most of the time I remember that—more than anything—I do not want to fight. Nobody wins. And worse, the biggest losers end up being my kids. That is the very last thing I want to see, so I work very hard and purposefully to find the high road, walk it, and choose my words very carefully. Most of the time saying nothing proves to be the best bet, but not always. Sometimes we have to have hard conversations, so we have them. We just agree to put on our big kid pants and find a solution that supports our child.

Other hiccups volunteer and usually when it's the worst timing.

When the random catastrophe happens, I find that I have to be gentle with myself. Owning my part in a miscommunication or other situation that goes sideways says more about one's character than all the good deeds and cheeriness of the good days combined. When I make a mistake, I work to understand my part, where I went wrong, and I genuinely apologize. Part of being a person guarantees the experience of screwing up—with and without intention. If I remember that and try to understand how and why something went awry, I gifted myself with the opportunity to grow and to be part of making it right again. When I live this way, I can walk with my head up knowing I have done my best to correct my mistakes. Once they're out there, there's no taking them back so making it as right as possible seems like something I can live with.

When I know my flaws, I have the opportunity to change those flaws. Some things I don't love about my personality simply exist in my DNA. I constantly work to improve those things about myself, but I also remember that I need to give myself the grace to be an imperfect person. When my feelings are really hurt or I feel attacked unjustly, I am most likely not in the space to execute my best self. The plan to act one way in response doesn't always play out as imagined or intended. Being alone in those times makes me feel a little bit more divorced than usual. I just have to remember that my marital status doesn't change my humanity.

So then what?

In owning my faults, I also need to own my gifts. If I activate the pieces of my personality I like as a means to overcome the aspects of my makeup I'd rather remove, I feed the good wolf, so to speak. The one I feed grows stronger–thanks to Matthew McConaughey's analogy that I'm sure he borrowed from someone else. Surviving the rough patches boils down to doing the work and training when the way is easy, and the burden is light. If I consistently work to be more of the person I want to become, then I find those positive, healthy habits easier to access and activate when the storms come. So, hope for sunshine but carry an umbrella because the flowers don't bloom without the thunderstorms.

POST CARD

My Self

C/O The Journey

What I learned from the Rd.

A Place, Startville

USA

A postcard to self of three positive things

Dear Self,

With Love, XXX

CHOOSE YOUR HEADING

You have survived the storm and look now for calmer waters and Steady Sailing with your kids page 62.

For introspection Page 12 Heading Out and Diving Deep.

Or stay on the path and follow our journey. Read on.

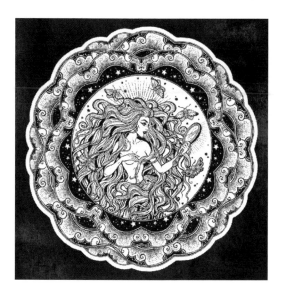

SELF LOVE ISLAND

The island stood alone surrounded by thousands of miles of open ocean. It seemed like the rest of the world was being kept at arm's length. From the water it looked wild and unkempt with its jungle growth spilling over its edges towards the dangerous jagged rocks surrounding it. No one except me would dare attempt a visit. Only I could get there and only I could decide how long I would stay.

Welcome to Self-Love Island

We all have our own private Self Love Island. We own it without paying a penny in rent. Some are large expansive islands, while others the size of a postage stamp. Some are barren, while others are covered with beautiful tended gardens. The size and care of our islands all depends on our length of visits and our purpose for visiting. Self-Love Island is a place where we see our true selves. We must learn to come to peace with that *self* or be doomed to never reaching our potential destination. Instead we sail in circles on shallow seas.

What is *Self-Love?*

Definition - regard for one's own well-being and happiness (chiefly considered as a desirable rather than narcissistic characteristic) Other synonyms - big headed, complacency, conceitedness, ego, pompousness, pride, pridefulness, self-admiration, self-assumption, self-conceit, self-congratulation, self-esteem, self-glory, self-importance, self-opinion, self-satisfaction, smugness, swell-headedness, vainglory, vainness. Antonyms - humbleness, humility, modesty.

Errrrrr. Nope... Well that is not at all the definition or purpose of adoration that we find on Self-Love Island. Going somewhere to just focus on yourself and ignore others or see ourselves above others is more a visit to self-pity. So why go there? I visit and return often as one of the greatest places of discovery and exploration. If I don't know where I am and what condition I am in, how do I know if I can move on?

Why go there? To explore myself and find balance by asking these important questions:

1. Where are you?
2. What do you want?
3. Where do you want to go?
4. How and when do you want to get there?

Without spending time pondering these great questions I will be on the lifeboat drifting aimlessly without a rudder. Most divorcees spend time in this drifting skiff. It's okay to float around, but at some point, I have to find myself on dry land. You may have asked these same questions on the beach before heading out on your new journey. I know I did. But I also found that as I journeyed, I grew. So, I come back and look in the mirror often. I notice the new gray hairs (unfortunately) and scars from issues I have fought with. I've lost some but won more as I continue forward.

I like the following definition of Self-Love - *"Self-love, self-respect, self-worth: There's a reason they all start with 'self.' You can't find them in anyone else."* ~ *Unknown*

During my visits I want to find hidden treasure or self-nuggets. No one can find these for you. They are buried deep or simply laying there on the surface, but you have to want to look with open eyes and heart. Be willing to take whatever you find and refine it to use on your journey. You can't dig up diamonds all the time. Sometimes it's an old rusty piece of metal that will require a lot of heat, refining, cleaning, and polishing. If you decide not to do the work and rebury or just leave your trash lying around, it will continue to corrode.

I've stared at a lot of junk on my island. There is plenty

to see without digging too deep. It is so easy to ignore and hide in what I think is a bottomless pit only to be sitting there like a lit billboard of the unmentionable. My junk yard is full of failed relationships and sad things that make me feel less of a person, mistakes that leave me not feeling whole. I've also felt ugly, overweight, and weak, but, more importantly, I have found that many of these memories and reflections are distortions. The ugly truths can also be used to create something that is better than it was before.

Simple Self-realization Facts That Come From Self Awareness

1. You can't love another if you can't love your reflection (with all the cracks and greasy thumbprints).

2. You can't compare your reflection to another's- It's yours as is your journey.

3. You can't find peace if you're still at war forgiveness is the best defense against anger and resentment.

4. Negative people don't hang around with positive. Surround yourself with positive people.

5. Love comes back when love and compassion are freely given.

6. You can't make room for healthy habits if you keep filling your trunk with junk.

7. Accept what you cannot love.

8. Never give up on yourself, your journey, or your loved ones.

Quick Trip or Permanent Vacation?

There are no fly-by trips. You can't pass over from 30,000 feet or make changes in a day trip. Coming to peace with yourself and your nuances takes time and continual work. Think of it like the gym. You may not want to go, but you know it is the only real way to get stronger, build muscle, and change how you look and feel. You can't go once, and you have to visit often and frequently. The same is for Self-Love Island. It takes a lot of tending and work.

How long is too long?

If you think sitting by a pool of reflection and having tears stream down your cheeks because of the love of your beauty is the goal... it's not. Having a healthy regard for one's own well-being and happiness is one thing. Having narcissistic characteristics and no regard for others is not the goal. The goal should be to get in and do the real work. Come to terms with self, be at peace with who you are at that moment and set positive goals for the person you want to become and the relationships you want to have.

Loving Yourself Benefits Those You Love

The Serenity Prayer: God, Grant me the serenity to accept the things I cannot change, the courage to change the things I can, and the wisdom to know the difference.

"You yourself, as much as anybody in the entire universe, deserve your love and affection." -Buddha

"Self-care isn't selfish--you can't pour from an empty vessel."-Eleanor Brown

One of my greatest strengths also happens to work itself out at times as my own downfall. I love people with everything I've got. I am passionate, I am extremely thoughtful, I prioritize the needs of those I love, and I desperately want to create a supportive, caring, and empowering blanket of support and protection around those people.

Sometimes I am so busy oozing love and caring that I forget to love on and care about myself.

Combining my creativity, thoughtfulness, and planning something special and meaningful to only that person is one way I show people they are important to me. This also means I am the world's worst secret keeper because I get so excited about whatever I've pulled together that I typically spill the celebratory beans.

I am a birthday party planning nut for exactly that

reason. As my daughter's first birthday approached, mostly adults and other babies filled the guest list, but I wanted her to look back and see the evidence of how crazy in love we were with her and how celebrating her short but remarkable emergence on the scene had transformed and brightened our lives. She looooooved Toy Story, so I made tiny cut out cowgirl hats with braided red yarn pigtails ending in diminutive pink satin bows on invitations that looked like a weathered Old West trail map to our house for a barbecue. (I literally tore and burned the edges so it would look like the Bonanza map.) I mean, we were Texans after all, and she looked adorable in her overalls. When my son turned four, he didn't leave the house without Thomas the Tank Engine in his hand, driving along the floor and shelves complete with choo-choo noises on imagined adventures unfolding everywhere from church to the grocery store. I made giant plywood cut outs of Thomas and his friends, turned our house into the Island of Sodor complete with painter's tape train tracks that led the preschoolers to different activities ending with decorating their own train-shaped cake and decked out in bandanas, engineer caps, and solving some problem just like Thomas would. When my at the time husband turned 30, I arranged for two friends to take him to a golf course he was dying to play with my dad, who is a scratch golfer. After their day at the course, I turned our outside deck into The 19th Hole, packed with our friends and his work friends to celebrate him. I made golf ball invitations delivered in what looked like fairway grass.

I thought out the details. I made sure the honoree had the time of their life doing exactly The Thing they loved without having to worry about anything else other than enjoying their celebration. I created magical experiences that were so personal to the people I loved that honestly blew them away.

I still do this, but it looks a little different because my kids are older and the people I care about need different things.

The effort, time, and work involved take first priority when I get into this mode. Christmas, birthdays, and special occasions kick my creative juices into full operational execution mode. There's nothing wrong with this. No one really expects it, and honestly, I think my kids find it kind of annoying these days. But when Mother's Day came and went the year things were starting to crumble without a card or even a verbal "Happy Mother's Day," to say it was a blow that leveled me would be an understatement.

I cut the crusts off the kids' PBJs every day. I made heart-shaped pancakes on Valentine's Day and every Saturday morning. Every special occasion and even sometimes just because it was Saturday were opportunities to show my family I adored them, and that Mother's Day, I stood over a pot of boiling water watching hard spaghetti soften into dinner because I thought surely we were going out to eat? Something?

I served that dinner to my husband and kids with tears in my eyes and a completely crushed heart. Then I excused myself from the table without eating, sat in the back of my closet and fell apart.

In those days, I found myself in the same spot in my closet many times for many different reasons feeling pretty much exactly the same horrible rejection over and over and over. I could not connect my effort to show my family how special they were, how I saw them as individuals worth celebrating for their unique characteristics with blatant inaction designed to let me know without a doubt that I was unimportant, valueless, and invisible.

During the time of our separation and divorce, my first priority was always my kids. This drastic catastrophic change to their lives would forever change everything for them, and I was partly at fault for causing it. I still believe without a doubt it was also best for us all, but that doesn't mean it was not sad or difficult. For a mom and wife so committed to bringing joy and sunshine to the lives of my family, willfully walking us into a hurricane felt wildly counterintuitive.

In the process of imagining how I could make the best of an awful situation, I sought out professional advice from a licensed therapist I admired. My initial reason for reaching out to her involved what I could do to protect and support my kids. Her answer surprised me.

The most important thing you can do is take care of yourself.

For once, I had no words, no questions, no comment.

What?

If you want your kids to handle this and go through it well, then you have to show them how. You have to take care of yourself, so you are healthy enough to take care of them.

OK. So what did that mean?

It meant so many things.
Eating, sleeping, yoga.
Friends, family and finding supportive people.
Dreaming big and envisioning my future.

Being spiritually strong and leaning on something

bigger than myself to carry me through my life.

Maintaining these things and prioritizing myself, finding balance, and saying no.

If you're like me, let's practice saying that word out loud: No.

In time, I found that I had scheduled these things into the times when my kids were gone. Like most newly single parents with kids, the drastic dichotomy in sound and activity level alone feels like a tremor in the parenting force when the kids exit with their dad. The silence was so loud, and the space grew so large and empty. Instead of withering in the lonesomeness of my kids' absence, these chunks of time became spaces full of opportunity to do something for myself. I scheduled yoga class on evenings the kids were with their dad and never missed. Instead of eating a microwaved can of soup, I reached out to a friend to meet me for dinner. I picked up hobbies long abandoned and finally bought a guitar. When I put the kids to bed each night, I filled the tub with bubbles and read the next chapter in a book. On my off weekends when it was just me, I found something to learn, experience, or see. I found whole weekends hardest to manage, so I made a list of everything I'd always wanted to visit or try that would require the majority of a day or more, put each on a tiny piece of paper, folded them up, and put them in a container. If a weekend approached with clear squares on my calendar, I'd choose one from the jar, and unfold my plans to execute right then--no excuses!

The unintended results paid off in building my confidence in tackling challenges I previously viewed as insurmountable. I challenged myself to put my money where my mouth was, quit using "someday" as an excuse, and had to idealize what life would look like if I actually believed I could do new things outside of my level of comfort. In the process, I met new people. I encouraged other people in similar situations who made their own lists of things to try. I expanded my repertoire of skills and interests. I also learned what things I never wanted to do again, and that was okay too. There's no shame in passing on an opportunity if I know it's not going to benefit me or build me up. My down time is too precious and too important to waste.

Over the years, the variables change, and they will continue changing. My kids are more independent. Relationships deserve varying amounts of my time. All of those are good things, but I have to maintain my commitment to caring for myself. If I'm run down, worn out, feeling like life is a marathon without water stations, I am headed for trouble or already in it without realizing my candle is burned out.

So, what does that look like a decade later?

Just like a car with a few miles on it, I need a tune up from time to time. Times of the year that get busy or require more emotional energy tend to be the times when I need to slow down and remember that I am not actually a superhero. When I stop and take a look at the quality of my responses in passing or notice that I can't turn my brain off at night because it's running with the list of to do's, I can usually draw a straight line to the fact that I've traded some of the things that keep me grounded for other things. Those other things are usually good and positive things--they are usually things like going somewhere with friends, something social, volunteering for something to do with my kids, or helping someone in a pinch. It's when missing me time becomes a habit that I find my responses are less personal, more distracted, not sincere. I notice that I slightly resent that I have so many things to do. I also realize that I usually need a hug and some encouragement. That's just me. I need those things, and it's OK to need those things. I just have to carve out the time to meet someone I know will encourage me for lunch. I have to say, "Hey, can I just have a hug?" Asking for what we need from the people who are invested in us is healthy. Snippy responses at red lights, not so much.

What's the plan for maintaining Team Me and all that comes with my vigorous life? Rest. Reflection. Being intentional about looking for the blessings in my life and being grateful for those things. Eating well, exercising, and stepping out into the sunshine for 5 minutes in the middle of a busy day. I write down the things I am grateful for and try to tell those people around me that I appreciate them. When I make sure I am healthy, I can better love those who make my life the richly beautiful playground it's become.

One more note on Mother's Day. So, the next year, I decided to plan lunch with the kids and my mom. I had them make her a card and explained why it was important, that she was important every day but that this was a special day to let her know we appreciated and loved her. They picked flowers from my garden to decorate the table, and I "helped" them bake a cake for her. In doing this, I modeled for them how to take a moment on special occasions to show people they are important. That day was quiet but sweet. I loved the simplicity of just being with my mom and with the two people I loved so fiercely. That night, my daughter walked into my bathroom with a plastic toy tray from her play kitchen. On it she carefully assembled cotton balls, a pink washcloth, the flowers from the table, and a small container of hotel lotion that smelled like gardenias. She made a tiny card that read Happy Mother's Day in pink crayon which also sat on the tray. Then she said she wanted to give me a pedicure for

Mother's Day.

This little girl gave me what she had to offer--not a gift she bought at a store or something anyone else took her to pick out. She filled the sink with warm water, carefully unfolded the washcloth, and patted the place on my vanity top where she wanted me to sit.

She washed my feet.

My eight-year-old daughter washed MY feet, all on her own without any prodding from anyone else. (If you think I'm not still crying as I write this, you are wrong!) I don't know where she got the idea, but I think it must have been from Sunday school. I sat there and choked back tears as her little hands dried my toes and smoothed the lotion on my calloused yoga feet with the cotton balls. Then I crushed her with an enormous hug and told her it was the best present I had ever gotten.

...You also should wash one another's feet. 15 I have set you an example that you should do as I have done for you. 16 Very truly I tell you, no servant is greater than his master, nor is a messenger greater than the one who sent him. 17 Now that you know these things, you will be blessed if you do them. - John 13:14-17 (NIV)

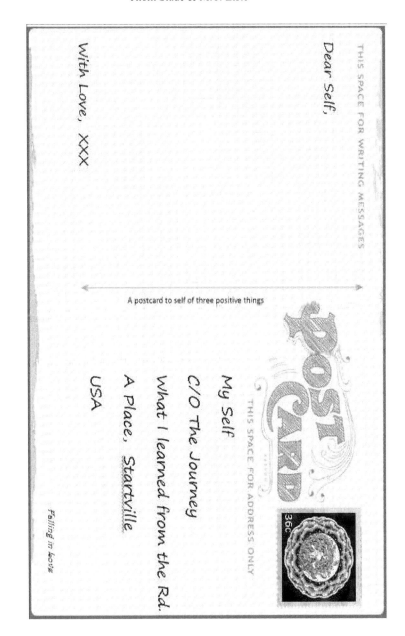

A postcard to self of three positive things

THIS SPACE FOR WRITING MESSAGES

Dear Self,

With Love, XXX

My Self

C/O The Journey

What I learned from the Rd.

A Place, Startville

USA

THIS SPACE FOR ADDRESS ONLY

POST CARD

36c

Falling in Love

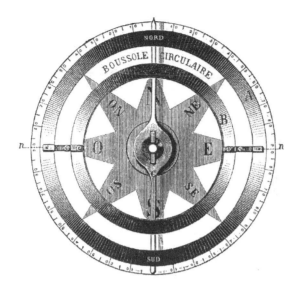

CHOOSE YOUR HEADING

Leaving the island, you feel ready to share your Self love and head to Wild Oats Island page 46.

Still feeling that you don't deserve love and respect you spiral down in a whirlpool to the Desert Island of Loneliness and Despair page 26.

Or stay on the path and follow our journey. Read on.

LOST AT SEA

It's been months and my boat has never looked better from the outside. I have scrubbed the decks, polished the brass, even ironed the flag, and then done it all over again. Day upon day, I complete the routine.

Scrub, polish, iron. Scrub, polish, iron.

I'm not sure why, as no one has seen it in months, and I have not let anyone aboard in a year. But everything sparkles against the ocean and moonlight. I man the tiller. I straighten my course and take care of business, but with no particular passion, no particular desire of destination, just the goal of moving forward and keeping it together. Scrub, Polish, Iron.

Busy Work

During the year or so it took to finalize my divorce, life felt uncertain and foggy. The year following it was still pretty much a "pea-souper" which is to say I felt quite lost in the sea of daily life and what my new non-married role was. The two things that seemed to make sense were the busyness of parenting and work. Keeping busy seemed to be the one thing that made things seem OK.

For the Love of Busy

As I was a complete marriage failure–or that is how I felt–I had this drive to succeed at other things. Maybe it was competitive parenting, but I threw myself into focusing on my kids, their activities, and school lives. In all of this, I lost some of myself but also found a new positive. I have always traveled for business. I have visited all 50 of our beautiful states and also worked for large international companies that have taken me around the world. I invested in my work during my marriage thinking it was for the long-term goal of urban success, or whatever that large white picket fence house in suburbia that I thought was a happy home. In some of that dream chasing I had missed a few school activities, birthdays, and parent interaction. Now I found myself involved everywhere, and I loved it. The normalcy and routine of making daily packed lunches helped paper over the cracks of loneliness and loss. It helped bring a beautiful, simple direction in a time of confusion and uncertainty. I became a master of simple quick meals, a lover of laundry, and punctual car pooler. In short, routines helped me have time to find joy in the simple things, find my family, and move on.

Dazed and Confused

See Jane. Jane is busy all day long. Jane never stops from sunup to sundown. Jane is a busy girl. Running at work, packed lunches, and PTA. Jane does it all, and Jane has no clue where or what she is really doing.

I will note that for as many people I have spoken to who had my experience, many other have found a new lease on life in their workplace, finding peace in extra hours at the office and a new zeal for the deal. For me at work, not so much. I have hired many people during my career, and I would not have hired myself during my divorce or the following 12 months. Don't get me wrong. I did not look like a homeless guy that had slept in a bush (that would be years later post match.com…) Scrub, polish, iron. I was well kept together on the outside, while inside I was a mess and definitely mid-bush sleeping. I just wasn't my driven creative self during that time. I longed for routine and home. Travel and work made me miserable. I lost many years to a company that gave nothing back, and I never felt I could give them my best. I was just distracted and lost.

Starting Again – Scrub, Polish, Iron

Over time, the fog in my work life began to clear and my passion, desire, and creativity returned. There was no rushing or charging ahead though the murk. The time lost was time to find self. Although I lost some direction in the workplace, I found more treasure in my home, family, and local community. Time is a great healer and fog lifter. I encourage anyone feeling a little lost at sea to slow down, enjoy the small things, fold some laundry, and polish some brass. Where you can't see the end of your nose today, your future will become clear and new opportunities will appear on the horizon.

Divorce & the Working Girl

Most of my friends who experienced divorce can't remember much about what they did at work that year. One blurred walk into the office, locate coffee pot, go to desk, figure out what to do next while managing the business of becoming divorced.

My experience was different because my work colleagues were also my ex-spouse's colleagues. We worked in the same organization, which meant something equivalent to living in a big small town. Each day as I pulled into the parking lot, I put on my badge and my game face, intentionally. Over my dead body was my work life going to fall apart like my marriage. Realizing I controlled how I handled myself, the minute I stepped through the front doors, I worked at working with passion, purpose, and the closest thing to perfection possible.

Two people in my office knew I was going through a separation and probably a divorce. I didn't tell anyone else on purpose. And neither did the people in whom I had confided. They understood when I needed to take a call or schedule a meeting during my lunch. Otherwise, no one knew anything was different in my world. Thank you to Mrs. Kingwell, my high school theater teacher!

Although I felt numb and terrified and desperately alone at home, I knew how to do my job and do it well. It was the place that felt normal, where I knew what to expect, where there weren't really any big surprises outside of the unknowns that come with the territory. It was the thing I could count on to be what it had always been. My one unchanging constant.

In the years since, I've earned more responsibility, expertise and knowledge, and added a couple of degrees to my CV. And I have the same job with the same title.

Divorce didn't send me into a stupor at work. It made me cautious.

When I became a one-income family responsible for a mortgage, day-to-day life, and two kids, I felt the gravity of my responsibility to hang onto stability. Divorce meant I haven't taken risks that I probably would have taken in a heartbeat if there was a second income supporting my family. It means that my kids have always come before my career. Always. It means that I turned down opportunities to make occupational moves that would have paid me more but required me to travel and be away from my kids with no back-up to care for them. It's meant staying in situations that are often thankless, ungratifying, not challenging, and without growth opportunity. And that's been my choice, 100 percent. And I wouldn't do anything differently given the chance because it's meant I could show up for my kids and be their present parent every day.

The trapdoor I avoid beckons me down a line of thinking asking me to flesh out my life if it had been different. If all of the *what if's* had worked in my favor and the hand life dealt me included a full house, what would my life look like today? Would I have more, be more, know more, accomplish more…. All things I can't possibly know. This is dangerous daydreaming territory too because there is no magical time eraser the change the last decade of my life or the one before that.

In my work life, this would equate to laying out a trove of excuses to explain away my lack of planning and execution of a project. I don't take that practice to work with me, and I don't let it materialize as a thought in my consciousness. In reality, my projects to manage are either completed and delivered or headed that way with deadlines a few years down the pipeline. Being present at work regardless of the stresses of my personal divergent travels on these seas has kept me pretty grounded. I'm proud of what I've been part of accomplishing in my work life. Who knows if those things would have materialized if I had been working in a different role.

As the end of high school is fast approaching for my oldest and those days are flying by for my youngest, I balance one foot on two piers–the one looking forward to my next adventures and the other, hanging on to savor every moment because these days are going fast.

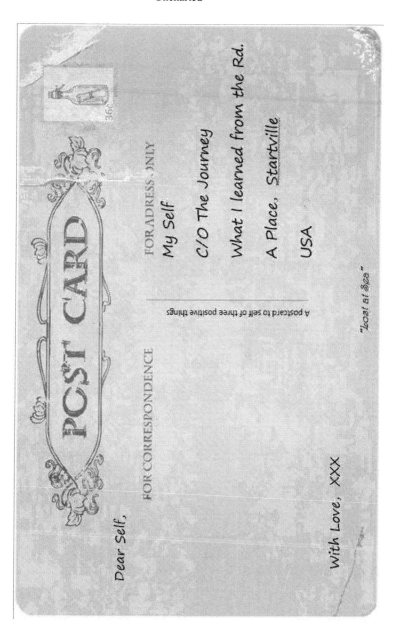

POST CARD

FOR CORRESPONDENCE

FOR ADDRESS ONLY

Dear Self,

My Self

C/O The Journey

What I learned from the Rd.

A Place, Startville

USA

A postcard to self of three positive things

With Love, XXX

"Lost at Sea"

360

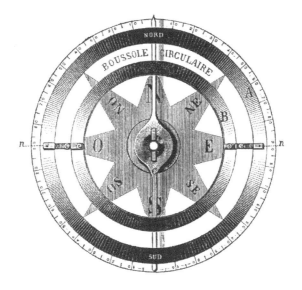

CHOOSE YOUR HEADING

The Lost has now been found and with confidence
heads out towards Wild Oats Island page 46.

Still feeling that you don't deserve love and respect
you spiral down in a whirlpool to the Desert Island of
Loneliness and Despair page 26.

Or stay on the path and follow our journey.
Read on.

DROWNING POST-DIVORCE

The divorce is final. You are free to chart your own course with the wind in your sails, anywhere your heart desires. So why then, are you gasping for air, struggling to stay afloat as the waves crash on your head? You go under again with what feels like your last breath.

Overboard

No matter the reason for how you got here, it was meant to be smooth sailing. So, what's the deal?

I came to America not on the Mayflower but as an exchange student. My eyes were wide and excited to meet Bon Jovi and "cheerleaders!" What I did not expect to meet was homesickness. One of the first school meetings off the boat was in a giant lecture hall where the dean warned us about the stages of leaving home, from euphoria to depression to eventually feeling settled. (He also warned us of "cheerleaders" which I unfortunately did not heed and resulted eventually in the telling of this story. Also note Bon Jovi was not at fault.)

I have never felt homesick. But low and behold in the middle of my college introduction of fun, one day it hit me–a sad feeling of missing the known. It took me by total surprise but in the 108-degree weather I actually missed the rainy gray cold of Northern England. I wrote some letters home and made some collect calls, but for a couple of weeks I felt very alone, lost, and adrift in an unknown sea.

Breathe and Go Down Again

It was the same way with my divorce. I would sail along, or at least move forward with my life in new direction, then wake up for no apparent reason swallowing water and gasping for breath. I felt out of my depth, lost, and quite alone with a longing to go home. No matter the grey gloom that I had sailed from, I wanted the normalcy of being home and married. My lack of buoyancy in my attitude meant I would have days where I was above water gasping at life and friends to then be followed by a day or two of underwater depression feeling heavy, like I could not breathe or go on.

Weight of the Past

The first year alone was of course the worst as I realized I was carrying the weight of my past and that of my ex. I look back now and see myself floundering in the water wearing one of those goofy fishing vests with a million pockets. Each pocket is weighed down with its own past memory, regret, or loss. Each weighing a ton. Some of the memories are like lures that hook my skin as I try to the remove them. Memories old, new, happy, sad, full of love, and also anger. They weigh heavy on my future by making me cling to my past.

Gasping, stressed out, underwater and under pressure, with family, friends, finances and expectations.

Learning to live free of self, guilt and the past (and the pressure of the future)

Slowly, over time I began to forgive the past and let go of unwanted weight. There was no quick fix, magical book, or sign up weight loss program. It was a conscious decision and still is years later. Sometimes it's day by day, moment by moment, pocket by pocket.

I learned that I cannot change the past, and the past can affect my future. Be calm and patient with yourself and those around you, and you will find yourself back in the boat breathing a little easier and moving on to your new adventure.

Ghost Stories of Relationships Past

No one wants to take a cruise on a haunted ship.

Ghosts of Relationships Past will haunt future relationships, unless you decide to stop running from the things you are afraid to face.

There wasn't a large amount of trust in my marriage and going through the process of a separation and divorce didn't exactly help. We would agree on one thing and then another would happen with alarming frequency. As a result, I struggle with worrying that I'm not always dealing with accurate information.

I also have a long history of losing people–sometimes by their choice and sometimes not–but the voided space where someone filled a part of my life feels kind of empty and like something precious is missing. I've lost friends, family members, my favorite pet… Loss is hard, and when my marriage ended, I lost the person who had truly been my best friend for a third of my life. For years, I didn't let anyone get close enough to leave a hole when they took off. Also, not a healthy solution or one I'd recommend.

When I finally started to stick my toe in the dating pool, I did so with a large amount of reluctance and a tiny smidgeon of hope. I believed my wounds had healed with time, and I'd built new relationships with people that looked like my vision of Healthy Adult Relationships. I reconnected with friends from childhood and college.

While I was pretty clear about my intentions–having just recovered from a large mistake, I was not looking to jump into a larger one–some people just don't listen. Or maybe they listen but think they can change my mind. Regardless, I ran into this pattern of men thinking that my agreeing to meet them for lunch to catch up somehow equated with this idea that I somehow immediately belonged to them. Like I was the Oreo and they licked it, so done deal. Seriously, this concept of "I found her first, she agreed to eat a salad across a table from me, so I'm calling dibs." *What?*

This did not resemble my vision of an Adult Relationship, healthy aside.

This happened a few times, and my response really puzzled me. It was a no-brainer that this mindset was absurd, but if this was what getting out there was like, no thanks, I'm good. I didn't like the pushiness, the complete disrespect for my boundaries, or the bulldozing plan of my life. You know, the one I had painstakingly built to protect myself and my kids and provide stability and consistency. This breed of single men was one I wanted no part of at all. Call me too independent, but this just felt slimy.

And it sent me back to a place where fear and hopelessness felt more comfortable, safer, than moving on.

I found myself jumping at what might be around the corner, just waiting for something to go "bump." This isn't who I had worked to become. It wasn't the example of resilience I wanted to model for my son and my daughter. And it wasn't really fun at all. I had work to do with the goal of figuring out why I let the actions and beliefs of other people define who I am.

I went back to many of the islands we talk about in this book. I looked for things I'd missed the first time (or the fourth time). I found myself reflecting from my current perspective in time and the experience under my belt that allowed me to look at things differently, with less emotion and more rationality. My first trip to look at my part equated with taking in a large-scale disaster. I was so overwhelmed by the effect of the whole that I didn't really notice the smaller aspects of the scene. I saw a painful, sad mess of destruction initially. This time, I saw the smaller, more specific instances where the little things I ignored or dismissed turned out to be the kindling that made the raging fire possible. So many little clues that things really were not what they had seemed in my life, and I either chose not to address them or I did but believed the excuses I received in response.

That was my part.

In owning that part, I gave myself the opportunity to grieve those things, to be mad at myself for being so stupid, to be mad at him for not being someone different (which isn't fair either). I looked those scary things in the face and realized the specters creating so much dread and fear of repetition in my present and future were just lies I let myself believe about days I hadn't lived yet. Remember specters are really just a lot of smoke and mirrors. The time had come to ask myself if there was really anything to be scared of.

Had I been hurt?

No.

Had I been taken advantage of?

No.

What was I so afraid of?

The answer was myself.

In realizing this, I understood something powerful about my choices. I can choose to spend my time anywhere. I can also choose not to spend my time just anywhere. If other people show me they are not trustworthy, that's information I need to make choices that are best for me and lead me in a direction I want my life to go. In the end I am the one who is responsible for my choices, and I have complete power to make basically any choice I want to make. When I take hold of that truth, the ghosts are quiet wisps of the past that has no bearing on my future unless I allow it.

You've done the work on yourself. Arm wrestled the demons of the past and grown into a better you. Things are looking up! Maybe you're ready to get back out there?

Proceeding with caution advised when entering new relationship territory.

I'm not a fan of the term falling in love. I don't think love is something one falls into. We grow to love someone in time with experiences of getting to know them in different situations and in discovering who they are. Relationships aren't about finding the perfect person then getting pelted with a cupid arrow. The real deal takes time and investment. Love is a verb. Love is a choice. Love is bigger than fear of things that aren't even real except in our imaginations.

Don't let the ghosts keep you chained in the past, missing the present and stealing the future.

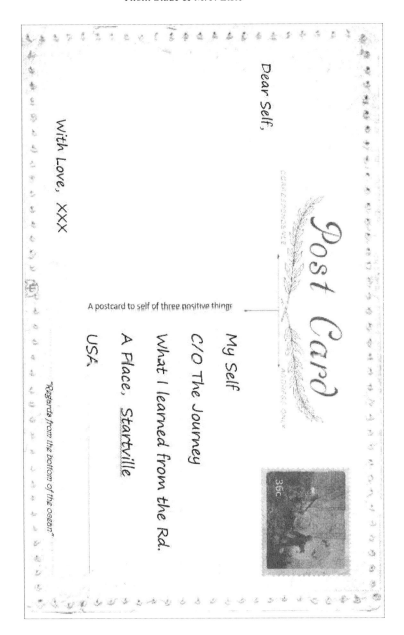

Dear Self,

With Love, XXX

Post Card

A postcard to self of three positive things

My Self
C/O The Journey
What I learned from the Rd.
A Place, Startville
USA

"Regards from the bottom of the ocean"

36c

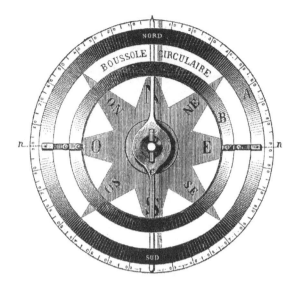

CHOOSE YOUR HEADING

You climb back in the boat, exhausted, cold and feeling sorry for yourself head to the Desert Island of Loneliness and Despair page 26.

For introspection Page 12 Heading Out and Diving Deep.

Or stay on the path and follow our journey. Read on.

YOU MADE IT! –
POST-DIVORCE NIRVANA

Divorce is not the end?

Pippin: I didn't think it would end this way.

Gandalf: End? No, the journey doesn't end here. Death is just another path, one that we all must take. The grey rain-curtain of this world rolls back, and all turns to silver glass, and then you see it.

Pippin: What? Gandalf? See what?

Gandalf: White shores, and beyond, a far green country under a swift sunrise.

Pippin: Well, that isn't so bad.

Gandalf: No. No, it isn't.

(from J.R.R. Tolkien Lord of the Rings)

Reaching the Shores of Your Nirvana

After years at sea, traveling to far off lands, visiting mysterious islands, and battling your own personal sea monsters, the goal of your destination appears on the horizon. You have been searching for months that have turned into years only to find that you have reached its golden shores. The waves gently lap the shore and welcome you back onto firm dry land. From your landing you see a path leading into the distance and on towards the crest of a majestic snow-capped mountain. Your destination, the goal of your journey, is in sight.

But before you pop the champagne, jump on the back of a white stallion to meet your new prince or princess, rein that pony in. Are you sure you made it to the right island, your final destination? There is a huge temptation along any difficult journey to set up camp when you find somewhere comfortable then the next thing you know you have a houseful of cats. I find this in my own life. I can get comfortable and forget my original intent. Why does this matter if I'm happy? Because settling for half your dream, half of what you can become, can lead back into unhealthy habits or relationships. So here I am. Ringing the bell for you on your last lap. It is time to push forward, to reach the goal that you set out to discover. For me this also highlights the importance of writing down my goals, setting my course and expectations back at the beginning of the journey on the beach. Before setting sail, before adventuring, define a life plan of where you are and where you want to get as a person, parent, and professional. So, as you land, check the landscape, and ask yourself:

Are you whole? Time to take stock.

The benefit of keeping a journal is to see how far you have come and grown as a person. Look back over your adventures and what at the time felt like near death experiences but today look like a point in time, something that happened and then it didn't. I remember the first day my divorce was final. It felt like my journey had ended. From today's perspective, I can see clearly that it was just an end of a chapter and a new adventure was beginning. Taking stock and looking at what has happened is an important part of self-reflection, in coming to terms with your new reality, and being at peace with:

✓ **Where you are today – Review your journey**

✓ **Reflecting but not dwelling on the past but moving on positively to your future – Look how far you have come**

✓ **Committing to continued growth as a positive person and a positive guide to those around you – Keep Moving Forward**

Do you need to travel and explore yourself, the past, or your goals? No problem. For once time *is* on your side. Taking time for yourself is never wasted time in the long run for yourself, others in your life, or those who will come into your life. (Just don't use it as an excuse to head back and build a house in Vegas.)

New relationships – Time to Rip Off the Band-Aids

As much as I like to preach the good word of relationship abstinence, especially for the first year following your divorce, I don't always practice what I preach. Doing the right thing and getting your house in order is hard work and not always a lot of fun. That's why we sometimes jump overboard and swim against the current in shark-infested waters towards the wild islands, even though we know it will end up with some kind of regret, tears, or bad rose tattoo. Taking time to get yourself and your house in order is the best long-term thing you can do for your future partner. There are no short cuts. For example, if you stick the 26.2 mile marathon bumper sticker on the back of your car when you really jogged to the pub on the corner and ate a pork-pie, bag of crisps, and 3 pints of beer, well you probably aren't ready for the real race. Same goes with a relationship.

On my journey I have traveled from –

- **soft and sobby**

   - **to holy mackerel that's what that feels like… to hell no!**

      - **to micro-picky dater (hand size and hair length deal killer, to oh, that's your favorite Christmas movie…)**

         - **to I'm "whole" being alone**

            - **to now I'm ready, ah wow, this is what a relationship is meant to feel like!**

In other words, it is another part of the journey. Expect some rocks.

The End. And the New Beginning

When you reach the beach and climb the hill following the sun as it rises over the mountains, find new shores, new lands, and new adventures. In all pain and suffering, understand that there is always another day. Another adventure awaits, but you have to open your door and set off on the path. You never know who you will meet and whose life you may change, join, or lift up.

Also, a warning of fires in the distance that look familiar. Do not repeat history.

My journey has been a long one, and I believe I'm ready to move on with the understanding the journey is not over. I encourage you to never give up on yourself, always remain positive, and keep yourself open to tomorrow. Even today new opportunities will cross your path.

Finding the Gumption to Move On

I'm not sure if gumption is an actual word.

It's something my East Texan family used as a way of saying you just have to dig deep and find the will to plunge ahead. That's 'gumption.'

So, I've been gumption mining for a while now. Many of us in this space are recovering from the most intimate of betrayals, and I still don't have definitive answers on how one gets over the betrayal of trust.

I'm positive I am not alone.

When we promise forever, meld our life with someone else's, and find something less than promising in the outcome, it's difficult to do the work to figure out how it came to this, how we move on, and how we trust someone else with our selves again. Physical intimacy aside, how do we let someone else see who we are, pull the defenses down, and reveal ourselves? How do we change our reality to a place where rejection isn't imminent?

So I did some research...

What do people need to recover from betrayal?

The breach lies in one's bank accounts--if you will--in the areas of trust and intimacy. In my view, those go hand in hand. You can't possibly have real intimacy without trust. Period. Some couples survive infidelity and pick Happily Ever After-ish. They picked Door Number 1. But what about those of us who find ourselves on the doormat staring at Door Number 2?

How do we move on to a healthy relationship? What happens when we feel threatened in that relationship? No one can blame us for feeling a bit gun shy, but where is the line of what makes sense and what is really in our imagination along the lines and boundaries that simply should not be crossed?

According to more than one expert, trust is built with someone not at all based on what they say but on what they do. Experts also agree that loving again is a slooooowwwwww process. (Like sloth running a marathon slow...) Since intimacy is dependent on emotional attachment, and emotional attachment pivots on the ability to trust, it looks like we have a bit of a challenge ahead of us.

Good News!

The good news is that recovery is a very real possibility. Understanding that building a bridge from both sides of the shore to mend the breach in trust is the first step in understanding the road to a trusting relationship. Two people can build a solid connection founded in trust. If it does not make sense, it may be that it does not make sense to you, but it is a place where the other person feels vulnerable. While vulnerability is a healthy thing, it also requires a space that is safe to BE vulnerable. In time, that space will grow, and becoming vulnerable gets easier because someone took the time and made the effort to become a safe place to be. So, the going there isn't as terrifying.

Dig deep. Choose to take the risks worth taking. It's out there. And completely worth it. I promise.

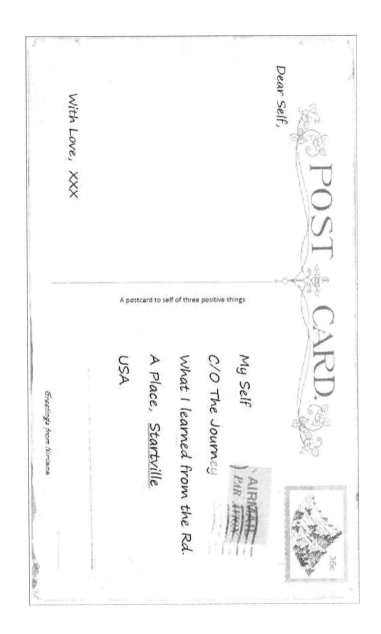

POST CARD.

Dear Self,

With Love, XXX

A postcard to self of three positive things

My Self

C/O The Journey

What I learned from the Rd.

A Place, Startville

USA

AIRMAIL
PAR AVION

36c

Greetings from Nowhere

REFERENCES

[i]https://www.thewildlifemuseum.org/exhibits/sharks/odds-of-a-shark-attack/

ABOUT THE AUTHORS

M.T. Lisle thought she married the perfect guy. Ten years later, she found herself alone with two children, a pile of debt, and a broken heart. Outside of her day job, you'll find her serving as her son's assistant robot inventor or cooking vegan desserts for her teenage daughter's friends. She's a passionate survivor of life's road bumps dedicated to continuously building on life's opportunities. A hopeless optimist, she invites readers into a candid look at her experiences in finding her way through divorce to a life richer than she imagined.

Thom Slade grew up in the North of England and met his wife of 17 years in college as an exchange student. He has been divorced and a single parent of three amazing kids for the last seven years. He is the founder of **IveMovedOn.com**, a community of therapists, lawyers and survivors of those going through and beyond divorce.

Made in the USA
Coppell, TX
14 November 2019

11345787R00087